# JAVASCRIPT & JQUERY

## STEP BY STEP TRAINING

Learn by doing step by step exercises.
Includes downloadable class files that work on Mac & PC.

## EDITION 2.7

Published by:
**Noble Desktop LLC**
594 Broadway, Suite 1202
New York, NY 10012
www.nobledesktop.com

# Table of Contents

# Table of Contents

# Table of Contents

# Table of Contents

## BONUS MATERIAL

# Table of Contents

## REFERENCE MATERIAL

# Downloading the Class Files

**Thank You for Purchasing a Noble Desktop Course Workbook!**

These instructions tell you how to install the class files you'll need to go through the exercises in this workbook.

---

## Downloading & Installing Class Files

1. Navigate to the **Desktop**.

2. Create a **new folder** called **Class Files** (this is where you'll put the files after they have been downloaded).

3. Go to **nobledesktop.com/download**

4. Enter the code **js-jquery-1611-04**

5. If you haven't already, click **Start Download**.

6. After the **.zip** file has finished downloading, be sure to unzip the file if it hasn't been done for you. You should end up with a **JavaScript jQuery Class** folder.

7. Drag the downloaded folder into the **Class Files** folder you just made. These are the files you will use while going through the workbook.

8. If you still have the downloaded .zip file, you can delete that. That's it! Enjoy.

---

# HTML vs. XHTML Syntax

---

## HTML vs. XHTML Syntax

HTML5 is the latest HTML web standard, offering flexibility, ease-of-coding, and powerful new features. An HTML5 document can be written using HTML or XHTML syntax. There are only minor stylistic differences between the two.

We prefer HTML syntax, which is what we'll use in this training. It's even a bit less typing! If you prefer to code using XHTML syntax, refer to the list below for the few XHTML differences:

- You must specify a document type at the top of the file.

- All tags must be in lowercase.

- All attributes must have quotes.

- All tags must have a close tag: `<p>this is a paragraph</p>`

- If tags do not have a close tag, such as a `<br>` or `<img>` tag, they must be written as self-ending: `<br />` or `<img src="image.gif" />`

---

# Before You Begin

## If You've Done Other Noble Desktop Coding Books

If you've setup Sublime Text in other Noble Desktop workbooks, the only new thing is that you need to install the **jQuery** package (instructions can be found below).

## Choosing a Code Editor to Work In

You probably already have a preferred code editor, such as **Sublime Text**, **Atom**, **Brackets**, etc. You can use whatever code editor you want, but if you don't have a preference we recommend **Sublime Text** (available for Mac and Windows). At **sublimetext.com** you can download a free trial. There is no time limit to the free trial, but if you like **Sublime Text**, you can purchase a copy for $70.

## Supported Browsers

In this workbook, we'll cover how to develop sites for modern browsers. If you discover something doesn't work in an older browser, you can often find workarounds if that browser is important to your audience.

## Recommended Software

**Sublime Text** is a great code editor for Mac and Windows. It has a free unlimited trial, which occasionally asks you to buy it. If you like it, you can buy it for $70.

Visit **sublimetext.com** and download the trial (or buy a copy) of **Sublime Text 3**.

We recommend installing some free packages (add-ons) that add great functionality. To make installing packages easier, you should first install **Package Control**.

### Installing Package Control

1. Launch **Sublime Text**.

2. Go into the **Tools** menu and choose **Install Package Control**.

3. After a moment you should see a message telling you that Package Control was successfully installed. Click **OK**.

### Installing the jQuery Package

The **jQuery** package install some helpful code snippets for working with jQuery Here's how to install it:

# Before You Begin

1. Open Package Control as follows:

   - Mac: Go into the **Sublime Text** menu > **Preferences** > **Package Control**.

   - Windows: Go into the **Preferences** menu > **Package Control**.

2. Choose **Install Package**.

3. In the list that appears, start typing **jQuery** and choose it when it appears.

4. A message in the bottom status bar will tell you when it's successfully installed.

## Installing the Emmet Package

**Emmet** offers shortcuts to make coding faster and easier. Here's how to install it:

1. After Package Control is installed, launch it as follows:

   - Mac: Go into the **Sublime Text** menu > **Preferences** > **Package Control**.

   - Windows: Go into the **Preferences** menu > **Package Control**.

2. Choose **Install Package**.

3. In the list that appears, start typing **emme** and **Emmet** should appear. Choose it.

4. A message will appear briefly in the bottom status bar to tell you it has been successfully installed.

## Installing the SideBarEnhancements Package

The **SideBarEnhancements** package will allow you to hit a keystroke to quickly preview a webpage in a browser. Here's how to install it:

1. Open Package Control as follows:

   - Mac: Go into the **Sublime Text** menu > **Preferences** > **Package Control**.

   - Windows: Go into the **Preferences** menu > **Package Control**.

2. Choose **Install Package**.

3. In the list that appears, start typing **SideBarEnhancements** and choose it when it appears.

4. A message will appear briefly in the bottom status bar to tell you it has been successfully installed.

## Setting Up F12 as a Shortcut for Preview in Browser

The **SideBarEnhancements** package, in addition to other things, lets you use **F12** as a keyboard shortcut for testing a webpage in a browser. To take advantage of this, you will need to add a little code to your Sublime Text preferences.

1. Go to **nobledesktop.com/sublimetext-shortcuts**

2. Copy the following code:

```
[
    { "keys": ["f12"], "command": "side_bar_open_in_browser" , "args":{"paths":
[], "type":"testing", "browser":""}}
]
```

3. In Sublime Text, open the key binding preferences as follows:

   • Mac: Go into the **Sublime Text** menu > **Preferences > Key Bindings**.

   • Windows: Go into the **Preferences** menu > **Key Bindings**.

4. A 2-column window will open. The **Default** key bindings are on the left, and **User** (your) key bindings are on the right. In the User key bindings on the right, select and delete any code that's there.

5. In the User key bindings on the right, paste the code you just copied.

6. We recommend previewing using Chrome because we like Chrome's Developer Tools. Add the following code highlighted in bold:

```
[
    { "keys": ["f12"], "command": "side_bar_open_in_browser" , "args":{"paths":
[], "type":"testing", "browser":"Chrome"}}
]
```

7. Save and close the file.

## Installing the AutoFileName Package

By default Sublime Text does not suggest path and filenames. Manually typing these is tedious and it's easy to make typos. The **AutoFileName** package adds much needed code hints as you're typing.

1. Open Package Control as follows:

   • Mac: Go into the **Sublime Text** menu > **Preferences > Package Control**.

   • Windows: Go into the **Preferences** menu > **Package Control**.

2. Choose **Install Package**.

3. In the list that appears, start typing **AutoFileName** and choose it when it appears.

4. A message will appear briefly in the bottom status bar to tell you it has been successfully installed.

## Restart Sublime Text

Some of the packages may require a restart. Quit and relaunch Sublime Text and you'll be all set!

## Recommended for Mac Users

You will need to test your website to make sure that it works in Microsoft Edge and Internet Explorer (IE), because these are some of the most popular browsers. They only run on Windows, so testing can be a challenge for Mac users. Luckily, there are virtual machines that will allow you to run Windows (and, therefore, test in Edge and IE) while you're still working on your Mac.

**VirtualBox** is a free application that runs Windows in a virtual machine side-by-side with Mac applications. It's an ideal testing environment because you can test in all Mac and Windows browsers. Visit **virtualbox.org** to download it and learn more.

Please note that Windows is not included with VirtualBox. You will need to download your own copy of Windows. Visit **tinyurl.com/windows-vms** to download free Windows virtual machines with Edge or IE pre-installed.

## Creating Your Own Copy of Class Files

Throughout this workbook you will be editing class files that we have prepared for you. Instead of editing the originals, we'll have you make a copy just for yourself to edit.

1. If you have any windows open, minimize or hide them so you can see the Desktop.

2. Open the **Class Files** folder.

3. Follow the appropriate Mac or Windows instructions below:

### Mac:

• Click once on the **JavaScript jQuery Class** folder to select it.

• Press **Cmd–D** to duplicate it.

• Rename the duplicate folder **yourname-JavaScript jQuery Class**.

### Windows:

• Click once on the **JavaScript jQuery Class** folder to select it.

• Press **Ctrl–C** to copy it.

• Press **Ctrl–V** to paste it.

• The new copy may be at the bottom of the list of folders. Rename it **yourname-JavaScript jQuery Class**.

4. You now have your own set of class files to use throughout the class. Have fun!

# Fundamentals of JavaScript Code

# 1B

## Exercise Preview

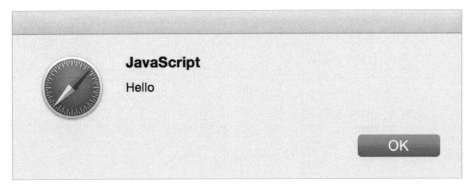

## Exercise Overview

Before we see real-life examples of how JavaScript is used, we must first learn some foundational concepts and syntax. First, you'll learn about alerts. You may not use them often on a finished website, but they're a useful way to test your code when you're first getting started. You'll then learn about variables, strings, and numbers. These are core concepts used throughout even the most complicated scripts.

## Getting Started

1. Launch your code editor (**Sublime Text**, **Dreamweaver**, **Atom**, etc.). If you are in a Noble Desktop class, launch **Sublime Text**.

2. In your code editor, hit **Cmd–O** (Mac) or **Ctrl–O** (Windows) to open a file.

3. Navigate to the **Desktop** and go into the **Class Files** folder, then **yourname-JavaScript jQuery Class** folder, then **JavaScript-Fundamentals**.

4. Double–click on **index.html** to open it.

5. Notice that this is just a blank HTML page. It will be the perfect canvas for us to start learning the syntax.

## Writing JavaScript Alerts & Variables

JavaScript code needs to be wrapped in a **script** tag, which we'll put in the **head** section.

1. Add the following bold code before the closing **</head>** tag (on line 6):

```
<title>JavaScript Fundamentals</title>
<script>

</script>
</head>
```

2. Inside the **script** tag, add the following bold code:

```
<script>
    alert('Hello');
</script>
```

**alert()** is a JavaScript **method** that will pop up a dialog containing whatever message you type into the parentheses. Methods can be thought of as the verbs of JavaScript. They are actions. They do things, like open an alert in this example. Methods are written as **methodName** followed by **parentheses** in which additional options are typically written.

3. Go to **File > Save**.

4. Navigate to the **Desktop** and go into **Class Files > yourname-JavaScript jQuery Class > JavaScript-Fundamentals**.

5. **Ctrl–click** (Mac) or **Right–click** (Windows) on **index.html**, go to **Open With** and select **Google Chrome**, **Safari**, or **Firefox**.

   NOTE: We do not recommend previewing in **Internet Explorer** (IE). For "security" reasons, Microsoft makes you manually allow JavaScript in local files! At the bottom of the window you must click **Allow blocked content**. It's important to know that this only happens locally and not on a live website. Because of this annoyance, we recommend previewing mostly with **Chrome**, **Safari**, and **Firefox**. Then occasionally, check **IE** to make sure it also works. (**Microsoft Edge** is better than IE because it no longer requires you to **Allow blocked content**.)

6. You should see a dialog that says **Hello**. Notice that it does **not** have quotes, even though there were quotes in the code. We'll explain that more in a moment. Click **OK** to close the alert.

7. Leave **index.html** open in the browser, so later you can reload the page to see the changes you make in your code.

8. Switch back to **index.html** in your code editor.

9. Make the following changes shown in bold. Pay close attention to capitalization—JavaScript is case-sensitive!

```
<script>
    var myMessage = 'Hello';
    alert(myMessage);
</script>
```

10. Let's break that down. The **var** in front of the variable name says we are declaring (or creating) a new variable. We made up a variable named **myMessage** into which we stored the message **'Hello'**. The alert is then told to display the contents of that variable. Notice that there are no longer quotes around the alert message.

11. Notice the **semi-colons** (;) at the end of each line of code. Semi-colons indicate the end of a statement. If multiple statements are on one line, then semi-colons must separate them. However, if they are on separate lines, JavaScript's official specs say that semi-colons are optional. This is a highly-debated topic, and some people leave them out. If you're ever going to minify your code (to reduce the file size) you'll need the semi-colons. Our personal preference is to use semi-colons, so we are going to add them in this workbook.

12. Go to **File > Save**.

13. Return to the browser and click the **Reload** button to refresh the new code. You should get the same **Hello** message. Click **OK** to close the message.

    NOTE: If you closed the file, navigate to **yourname-JavaScript jQuery Class > JavaScript-Fundamentals** and **Ctrl-click** (Mac) or **Right-click** (Windows) on the file, then select **Open With** and choose your favorite browser. Alternatively most code editors have a shortcut to make previewing a page in a browser easier (some are shown below).

---

**Browser Preview Shortcuts**

If you are using Sublime Text with **SideBarEnhancements** installed and have set your user key bindings in the **Before You Begin** section at the beginning of the workbook, hit **F12** (or **fn–F12** depending on your keyboard settings) to open the saved HTML document in your default browser.

This typically does not work on a Mac unless you disable/change the **Show Dashboard** keyboard shortcut in **System Preferences > Mission Control** (or **Keyboard**).

If you are using Dreamweaver, go to **File > Preview in Browser**.

---

14. Back in your code editor, put **single quotes** around **myMessage** in the alert, as shown below:

```
alert('myMessage');
```

15. Save the file and preview in a browser. Now the alert should say **myMessage**.

This text within quotes is called a **string**.

Quotes are important because they tell JavaScript that text should be read literally as a string of characters. If there are no quotes, JavaScript understands it's not just a series of characters, but a variable. JavaScript doesn't care about single vs. double quotes. It's mostly a personal preference (except in a few cases). We prefer single quotes because they're faster to type because you don't have to hold the Shift key!

16. Switch back to your code editor.

17. We don't need this code anymore because we're moving on to something else. We'd like to keep the code in the file, but have it ignored by the browser. As shown below, add double slashes **//** to comment out the code (it will turn gray).

```
//var myMessage = 'Hello';
//alert('myMessage');
```

18. Save the file and preview in a browser. The alert code is ignored, so nothing will happen.

## Strings vs. Numbers & Variables

1. Let's further explore how quotes work. Switch back to your code editor.

2. Below the commented lines, type:

```
   //alert('myMessage');
   alert( 2 + 2 );
   alert( '2' + '2' );
</script>
```

3. Save the file and preview in a browser.

- The first alert is doing basic math. The plus is working as an addition sign. Click **OK** to see the second alert.

- The second alert is doing something different. The quotes indicate a string. The plus sign is now putting one string of characters after another (a process called **concatenation**). Click **OK** to close the alert.

4. Back in your code editor, delete everything between the **script** tags.

5. Add the following bold code:

```
<script>
   var firstName = 'Dan';
   var lastName = 'Rodney';
   alert('firstName' + 'lastName');
</script>
```

6. Save the file and preview in a browser. The alert will say **firstNamelastName**. Click **OK** to close the alert.

   The quotes in the alert treat those words as strings, or as literal characters. We've concatenated (or combined) these two strings. But that's not what we want.

7. Switch back to your code editor.

8. Remove the quotes in the alert:

```
<script>
    var firstName = 'Dan';
    var lastName = 'Rodney';
    alert(firstName + lastName);
</script>
```

9. Save the file and preview in a browser. The alert will say **DanRodney**. Click **OK** to close the alert.

   Without quotes, JavaScript treats **firstName** and **lastName** as variables, so it looks for their value outside the alert. There were no spaces between the names in the alert. To output a space, we'll need to concatenate a string (containing a space character) between the **firstName** and **lastName** variables.

10. Switch back to your code editor. Add the following **quote space quote space plus** shown in bold:

```
alert(firstName + ' ' + lastName);
```

    NOTE: Spaces outside the quotes don't matter, but spaces inside the quotes do!

11. Save the file and preview in a browser.

12. Notice that it now outputs **Dan Rodney** (with a space). Click **OK** to close the alert.

13. In your web browser, close the page.

    These examples may seem basic, but they are laying a very important foundation for the more complex scripts you'll soon be writing.

    NOTE: For each exercise in this book, we have the completed code in a folder named **Done-Files**. Go to **Desktop > Class Files > yourname-JavaScript jQuery Class > Done-Files > JavaScript-Fundamentals** if you want to refer to our final code.

## Exercise Preview

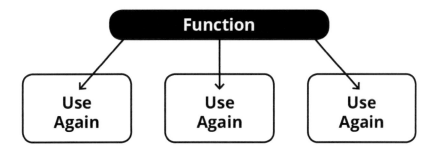

## Exercise Overview

A **function** is a group of reusable code that performs a specific task (or tasks) at a desired time. The function can be run repetitively, potentially using different information each time it runs. Methods such as **alert()** are similar to functions, but they're predefined. We can do multiple alerts with varying text, but it's essentially doing the same task again. Functions, however, are defined by you. You decide what they will do, so in this exercise, you'll learn how to make a custom function.

---

## Defining Functions

1. Open your code editor if it isn't already open.

2. Close any files you may have open.

3. In your code editor, hit **Cmd–O** (Mac) or **Ctrl–O** (Windows) to open a file.

4. Navigate to the **Desktop** and go into the **Class Files** folder, then **yourname-JavaScript jQuery Class** folder, then **Functions**.

5. Double–click on **index.html** to open it.

6. Add the following bold code before the closing **</head>** tag (on line 6):

   ```
   <title>Functions</title>
   <script>

   </script>
   </head>
   ```

7. In the **script** tag, add the following bold code to define a function:

   ```
   <script>
       function displayName() {
           alert('Dan Rodney');
       }
   </script>
   ```

8. Let's break this down. We just declared a function named **displayName()**. The function will perform everything between the curly braces **{ }**, which is to **alert()** the name **Dan Rodney**. Keep in mind that JavaScript is case-sensitive. We used a capital N for our function's name, **displayName()**. Later we'll need to match that case or else things could break.

9. Save the file.

10. Preview **index.html** (from the **Functions** folder) in a browser.

   NOTE: Most code editors have a way to make previewing a page in a browser easier, such as the **F12** shortcut in Sublime Text with the SideBarEnhancements package installed or **File > Preview in Browser** in Dreamweaver.

   If your code editor doesn't have one, you can always open the pages from your browser window to preview it. In your browser, you can hit **Cmd–O** (Mac) or **Ctrl–O** (Windows) to open **index.html**. Navigate to the **yourname-JavaScript jQuery Class** folder and then **Functions** to find the file.

11. Notice that nothing happens. Code inside functions is only executed when the function is called. Let's see how to do that.

12. Leave index.html open in the browser, so you can reload the page to see the changes you make in your code.

## Calling Functions

1. Switch back to your code editor.

2. We want to run this function when the user clicks a button. In the **body** section, type the following text in bold:

```
<body>
    <button>Show a Name</button>
</body>
```

3. Now we need the button to "talk" to JavaScript. HTML elements do not listen for events by default. Instead, we need to tell them to listen for events (such as the click of a button). Here we'll add the **onclick** attribute and set it equal to the function we want to trigger. Add the following bold code:

```
<body>
    <button onclick="displayName();">Show a Name</button>
</body>
```

   NOTE: Adding **onclick** will tell the button to listen for a click event, and only execute the code within the function at that time. The onclick **event handler** is one of many, and we'll see more in the coming exercises.

4. Now when the user clicks the button, our **displayName()** function will run. Let's check it out. Save the file and preview in a browser.

5. Click the **Show a Name** button. An alert should appear with the name Dan Rodney in it. Click **OK** to close the alert, then click the button again to see that the alert appears again. We're reusing the code!

## Defining Parameters & Passing Arguments

1. An alert that always displays the same thing isn't very flexible. Let's make it work with different names. Switch back to your code editor.

2. In order to make a function reusable, we give it **parameters**. Then when we call the function, we can pass information into it. Around line 7 add these two parameters to the function:

```
function displayName(firstName, lastName) {
    alert('Dan Rodney');
}
```

3. Now edit the alert to use those parameters:

```
function displayName(firstName, lastName) {
    alert(firstName + ' ' + lastName);
}
```

4. While a function's **parameters** ask for information, the pieces of info we pass to it are called **arguments**. Below, change the button to pass the arguments **'Dan'** and **'Rodney'** to the **displayName()** function.

```
<button onclick="displayName('Dan','Rodney');">Show a Name</button>
```

IMPORTANT! Notice that Dan and Rodney are surrounded by single quotes, not double quotes. JavaScript doesn't care which are used, but HTML does. For HTML, the double quotes must wrap the onclick attribute's value. If we used double quotes, HTML would think the onclick attribute would end too early and things would break.

5. Save and preview **index.html** in a browser.

6. Click the **Show a Name** button. Again, it should alert **Dan Rodney**, but this time those names were passed into the function.

7. Click **OK** to close the alert.

8. Switch back to your code editor.

9. Make a second button by copying and pasting the first one.

```
<button onclick="displayName('Dan','Rodney');">Show a Name</button>
<button onclick="displayName('Dan','Rodney');">Show a Name</button>
</body>
```

10. Alter the second button so it looks as shown below:

```
<button onclick="displayName('Dan','Rodney');">Show a Name</button>
<button onclick="displayName('Trevor','Sammis');">Another Name</button>
```

11. Save and preview the file in a browser.

12. Click each of the buttons. They should give you two different alerts. That is one flexible function!

    NOTE: If you want to refer to our final code example, go to **Desktop > Class Files > yourname-JavaScript jQuery Class > Done-Files > Functions**.

    _____

## Exercise Preview

## Exercise Overview

In this exercise, we'll take a look at what JavaScript is doing in the background. We'll use Chrome's DevTools to reveal the structure of the HTML document. We'll select individual HTML elements and change them using JavaScript.

---

## Getting Started

1. On your Desktop, navigate into **Class Files > yourname-JavaScript jQuery Class > Form-Fields** folder.

2. We want to use Chrome's Developer Tools (DevTools), so we'll open our page in Chrome. **Ctrl–click** (Mac) or **Right–click** (Windows) on **form.html** and choose **Open With > Google Chrome**.

3. **Ctrl–click** (Mac) or **Right–click** (Windows) anywhere on the page and choose **Inspect** from the menu.

4. We can now see Chrome's DevTools. All modern browsers have Developer Tools. We can diagnose problems here and see what the browser is doing. We can also see all of the HTML, CSS, and JavaScript that the browser is reading.

5. The DevTools window has several groups of tools organized into tabbed panels. By default, you should see that the **Elements** panel is open.

   In the **Elements** tab you can inspect an HTML element and see its precise markup. Mouse over any of the lines of HTML. As you do so, you should see the corresponding element highlighted in the browser window.

6. At the top left of the DevTools window, click the ⧉ button. Now when you mouse over an element in the page, the corresponding HTML highlights in DevTools.

7. Click the ⧉ button again to turn this off.

8. At the top of the DevTools window, click on the **Console** tab.

   If there are JavaScript errors in the page, we will see them here. The Console is also a place where we can experiment safely with JavaScript.

9. In the Console, type **alert('Hello');** and hit **Return** (Mac) or **Enter** (Windows).

10. You should see a dialog that says **Hello**. Click **OK** to close the alert.

11. The Console lets us make temporary changes to the HTML page we're looking at (even a working site). We're going to experiment with hiding and showing various parts of this page.

    Type **document** into the Console and hit **Return** (Mac) or **Enter** (Windows).

12. You should see **#document** return in the Console. Mouse over the word **#document** and notice that the whole page is highlighted.

13. Click the **arrow** next to **#document** to expand it. This is the whole HTML document, and contains everything on the page.

14. Click the **arrow** next to **<body>** to expand it, and see all of the contents of the body.

15. Mouse over the various sections inside the **<body>** and notice that those blocks of content highlight in the browser.

---

## Selecting & Working with HTML Elements

We don't typically want to make changes to the whole **document** all at once. We want to specify which HTML element we'd like to change. To get more specific, we can use the JavaScript method **document.getElementById()**. This **dot syntax** will become more familiar as we continue to dig deeper into accessing elements and their different properties as we go through the exercises.

1. At the top left of the DevTools window, click the ⧉ button.

2. In the page, click on the text field under **Name**.

3. In the DevTools, notice that the input with the ID **nameField** is highlighted.

4. In the DevTools, click on the **Console** tab.

5. In the Console, type **document.getElementById('nameField');**

> ### About getElementById()
>
> The **getElementById()** method allows you to target any HTML element in the document by placing its ID as a string inside the method's parentheses. Please note that the capitalization of **Id** in the name of this method must be correct for the code to function. However tempting it may be to write getElementByID(), the function will not work written this way.

6. Hit **Return** (Mac) or **Enter** (Windows).

7. You should see **<input id="nameField ... value="First and Last Name">** in the Console.

   Mouse over this and notice that only the nameField input highlights. So far we've selected the whole element whose ID is **nameField**. We can get more specific and talk to this element's styles by using dot syntax again.

8. To save yourself some typing, press the **Up Arrow** key in the Console. This will show your last command so you don't have to type it again. Very handy!

9. Add the following bold code to this previous command:

   document.getElementById('nameField')**.style.display = 'none';**

   This statement says to get the element with the ID **nameField** and set its **display** property to **none**, which will hide the input. Note that the property value ('none') must be a string.

10. Hit **Return** (Mac) or **Enter** (Windows) to execute the code and notice that the input disappears!

11. Let's get the nameField to reappear. In the Console, press the **Up Arrow** key again to show your last command.

12. Change the code as shown in bold:

   document.getElementById('nameField').style.display = **'block';**

13. Hit **Return** (Mac) or **Enter** (Windows). The input should reappear.

---

## Getting & Setting Input Values

Inputs are special elements that we can use to collect information from our users. HTML **input** elements have a **value** attribute that changes when data is entered into the input. Let's get and set the value of one of the inputs on this page.

# 1D  Targeting HTML Elements

5. Type the following into the Console:

   **document.getElementById('nameField').value;**

6. Notice that the Console returns the text **"First and Last Name"**. This is the current value of the input tag.

7. Let's change the value to something else. On the page, click into the **Name** field and replace the text with your own name.

8. Let's see how JavaScript can **get** the new value of the input. Click on the Console to put your cursor there.

9. Press the **Up Arrow** key to show your last command.

10. Hit **Return** (Mac) or **Enter** (Windows) to execute the code.

11. Notice that the Console should return the new value—your name!

12. We can also use JavaScript to **set** the value of an input. Press the **Up Arrow** key again to show your last command.

13. Make the following changes shown in bold:

    document.getElementById('nameField').value **= 'example: John Doe';**

14. Hit **Return** (Mac) or **Enter** (Windows) to execute the code.

15. Notice in the page that the text field below **Name** should now say **example: John Doe**.

16. Code written in the Console will be lost when we refresh the page. Click the browser's **Reload** button to see that your changes are gone.

    While changes made in the Console are not permanent, it's a great way to test small pieces of code.

___

## Exercise Preview

## Exercise Overview

There are times when you only want your JavaScript code to be executed if certain criteria have been met. We can test for those criteria, and then execute code if the criteria are true. These are called **conditional statements**. In this exercise, we'd like to include placeholder text in our form fields. Users shouldn't have to delete the placeholder to enter text into the form field. We'll detect whether the form field has text in it (or not) and have our JavaScript respond appropriately.

## Getting Started

1. Open your code editor if it isn't already open.

2. Close any files you may have open.

3. For this exercise we'll be working with the **Form-Fields** folder located in **Desktop > Class Files > yourname-JavaScript jQuery Class**. You may want to open that folder in your code editor if it allows you to (like Sublime Text does).

4. Open **form.html** from the **Form-Fields**.

5. Preview the page in a browser. This is the same page you worked with in the previous exercise.

6. Leave the page open in the browser so we can come back to it later.

7. Switch back to your code editor.

8. We want to clear the initial text from the **Name** text field when the user clicks or Tabs into it. We'll need a function to make sure it doesn't happen on page load. Let's first call that function by adding an **event handler**.

   Add the following bold code to the **nameField** input tag on line 25:

   ```
   <input id="nameField" name="nameField" type="text" class="textfield"
   value="First and Last Name" onfocus="clearName();">
   ```

   NOTE: **onfocus** is similar to **onclick**, but is better in this case. **onclick** would only work if the user clicks with a mouse. **onfocus** works when the object becomes focused on (or highlighted). That means it's triggered by mouse clicks as well as users Tabbing into the field via the keyboard.

9. Now let's define that function. Add the following bold code before the **</head>** tag (on line 8):

```
<link rel="stylesheet" href="css/main.css">
<script>

</script>
</head>
```

10. We already told our HTML to listen for an onfocus event and trigger a clearName() function at that time. Now, we'll create the function that will be triggered.

    In the **script** tag, add the following bold code:

```
<script>
    function clearName() {

    }
</script>
```

11. We saw in the previous exercise that we can successfully talk to the text field, and get and set input values using JavaScript. We'll use the same **getElementById()** method. Add the following bold code.

```
function clearName() {
    document.getElementById('nameField').value = '';
}
```

    At the end of the line we have a pair of single quotes with nothing between the quotes. That means the text field's text will be set to nothing.

12. Save and reload **form.html** in Chrome.

13. Click into the **Name** field (or Tab into it). The default text should disappear.

14. Type your name into the **Name** field and then click (or Tab) into the **Phone** field.

15. Click (or Tab) back into the **Name** field to change the name. Whoops, the text disappeared again. What if someone makes a typo they need to correct? They'd have to retype the whole thing. How annoying! Let's fix that.

---

## Using If Statements

We need to add a conditional statement, which is a bit of logic that will only execute some code if a specific condition is met.

1. Switch back to your code editor.

2. The text should only be cleared if it says the default **First and Last Name**. Wrap the line into an **if** statement, and don't miss the end curly bracket!

```
function clearName() {
    if () {
        document.getElementById('nameField').value = '';
    }
}
```

3. Copy and paste the **nameField** line without the semi-colon into the **if** statement's parentheses, as shown in bold below.

```
function clearName() {
    if (document.getElementById('nameField').value = '') {
        document.getElementById('nameField').value = '';
    }
}
```

4. Change the **if** statement's equal sign to a **double** equal sign as follows. One equal sign **sets** something equal to something else (so a change is happening). Two equal signs **check** to see if the values on either side of the **==** are already equal. It's a test that returns **true** or **false**.

```
if (document.getElementById('nameField').value == '') {
```

5. In the **nameField** input tag around line 31, copy the value **First and Last Name**.

6. Paste it into the **if** statement:

```
if (document.getElementById('nameField').value == 'First and Last Name') {
```

NOTE: We highly recommend copying and pasting things like this because even the best of us make typos. A simple typo can produce unexpected errors, making you waste a lot of time trying to figure out what's wrong with a script. Copy/Paste can help you avoid that!

7. Save the file, switch to the browser, and reload **form.html**.

8. Type your name into the **Name** field.

9. Click out and back into the **Name** field. It doesn't disappear any more. That's because we only clear the value if the value is equal to the initial text. Perfect.

10. Switch back to your code editor.

11. We want a similar function for the phone number, so let's just duplicate the clearName() function and make a few corrections. Select and copy the entire **clearName()** function, including its ending curly braces.

```
function clearName() {
   if (document.getElementById('nameField').value == 'First and Last Name') {
      document.getElementById('nameField').value = '';
   }
}
```

12. Paste a copy directly below it.

13. Edit the code you pasted, changing **name** to **phone** in three places as shown below in bold. Pay close attention to capitalization!

```
function clearPhone() {
   if (document.getElementById('phoneField').value == 'First and Last Name') {
      document.getElementById('phoneField').value = '';
   }
}
```

14. In the **phoneField** input around line 39, copy the value **example: 212-123-1234**.

15. Paste it into the clearPhone **if** statement:

```
if (document.getElementById('phoneField').value == 'example: 212-123-1234') {
```

16. Add the **onfocus** call to the **phoneField** around line 39:

```
<label for="phoneField">Phone:</label>
<input id="phoneField" name="phoneField" type="text" class="textfield"
   value="example: 212-123-1234" onfocus="clearPhone();">
```

17. Save the file, switch to the browser, and reload **form.html**.

18. Test out the two fields. They will only clear when they have the default values.

---

## Reshowing Text Hints in Empty Form Fields

Currently, when we click into a field, JavaScript removes the text. That's nice, but if the user clicks into another field without entering any text, it would be nice if the initial text would reappear.

1. Switch back to your code editor.

2. Select and copy the entire **clearName()** function around line 9 shown below:

```
function clearName() {
   if (document.getElementById('nameField').value == 'First and Last Name') {
      document.getElementById('nameField').value = '';
   }
}
```

3. Paste a copy directly below the one you just copied.

4. In the bottom copy you just pasted, change **clearName** to **resetName** as shown:

```
function resetName() {
```

5. If the text field is empty when the user clicks or Tabs out of it, we want to reset it back to the initial text. In the **resetName()** function, cut the **First and Last Name** from the **if** line and paste it into the line below, so you end up with:

```
function resetName() {
    if (document.getElementById('nameField').value == '') {
        document.getElementById('nameField').value = 'First and Last Name';
    }
}
```

6. Next we must call our new function. Add the following to the **nameField** (around line 41):

```
<input id="nameField" name="nameField" type="text" class="textfield"
value="First and Last Name" onfocus="clearName()" onblur="resetName();">
```

NOTE: **onblur** is the opposite of **onfocus**. **onfocus** is when the cursor is put into the text field, so **onblur** is when the cursor is removed from the text field (such as when the user clicks or Tabs into the next field).

7. Save the file, switch to the browser, and reload **form.html**.

8. Click or Tab into the **Name** field to see the text disappears. Then click or Tab into the **Phone** field and see the initial text reappear in the Name field. Great!

9. Switch back to your code editor.

10. Select and copy the entire **clearPhone()** function shown below:

```
function clearPhone() {
    if (document.getElementById('phoneField').value == 'example: 212-123-1234') {
        document.getElementById('phoneField').value = '';
    }
}
```

11. Paste a copy directly below the one you just copied.

12. In the bottom one you just pasted, change **clearPhone** to **resetPhone** as shown:

```
function resetPhone() {
```

13. In the **resetPhone()** function, cut the **example: 212-123-1234** from the **if** line and paste it into the line below, so you end up with the code shown below:

```
function resetPhone() {
    if (document.getElementById('phoneField').value == '') {
        document.getElementById('phoneField').value = 'example: 212-123-1234';
    }
}
```

14. Next we must call our new function. Add the following to the **phoneField** around line 49:

```
<input id="phoneField" name="phoneField" type="text" class="textfield"
value="example: 212-123-1234" onfocus="clearPhone()" onblur="resetPhone();">
```

15. Save the file, switch to the browser, and reload **form.html**.

16. Click or Tab between the **Name** and **Phone** fields. Their initial text should disappear when the cursor is there but reappear when you click to the next field. But if you type a name or phone number, that will remain instead of the initial text hint.

   NOTE: If you want to refer to our final code example, go to **Desktop > Class Files > yourname-JavaScript jQuery Class > Done-Files > Form-Fields**.

   **HTML5 Placeholder Attribute**

   HTML5 added a new **placeholder** attribute that has similar functionality to what you just created with JavaScript. Even if you use the HTML placeholder instead of JavaScript, you still learned some very useful concepts in this exercise.

## Optional Bonus: Adding a Third Form Field

Use what you've learned to create a third form field to collect an **email address**:

- You'll need to add HTML (similar to the existing HTML for the first two form fields). Feel free to copy and paste!

- You'll need to add JavaScript (similar to the existing functions that work on the first two form fields).

Simple Accordion with JavaScript

## Exercise Preview

## Exercise Overview

Accordions let you condense a lot of information into a small space by hiding some of it. One click and another section appears, covering over the previous section. In this exercise, you're going to build a simple accordion using JavaScript to hide and show different elements.

## Getting Started

1. Open your code editor if it isn't already open.

2. Close any files you may have open.

3. For this exercise we'll be working with the **Simple-Accordion** folder located in **Desktop > Class Files > yourname-JavaScript jQuery Class**. You may want to open that folder in your code editor if it allows you to (like Sublime Text does).

4. Open **index.html** from the **Simple-Accordion** folder.

5. Preview the page in a browser.

6. Notice that there is an accordion on the right side of the page. The accordion has three "panels" that list different types of events. Each panel is made up of a tab at the top and some content below. When the user clicks on one of the tabs we want to show that tab's content and hide the other panels' content.

7. Click on one the accordion's tabs (such as **Coming Up**) to see that the hiding/ showing is not working yet.

8. Leave the page open in the browser so we can come back to it later.

9. Switch back to your code editor.

10. Add the following bold code before the closing **</head>** tag (on line 7):

```
<link rel="stylesheet" href="css/main.css">
<script>

</script>
</head>
```

11. Let's write some JavaScript to hide the two bottom panels. We want to hide the content portion of each panel. They are in divs called **comingUpContent** and **pastEventsContent**.

    Let's start by hiding **comingUpContent**. We need to target it so JavaScript knows which element to work on. Inside the **script** tag, type the following bold code:

```
<script>
    document.getElementById('comingUpContent');
</script>
```

12. We will access a CSS property for the element using JavaScript's dot syntax. Type the following bold code:

```
<script>
    document.getElementById('comingUpContent').style;
</script>
```

13. Let's continue to use dot syntax to specify which CSS style we wish to modify, and the new value we'd like to set:

```
<script>
    document.getElementById('comingUpContent').style.display = 'none';
</script>
```

    The **HTMLElement.style** property allows us to access and modify the element's **style** attribute. Since the **style** property has the same (and highest) priority in the CSS cascade as an inline style declaration, it is useful for modifying the style of one specific element and will allow us to override the external style sheet.

14. Save the file, switch to the browser, and reload **index.html** to see that nothing happens. We wanted to hide the **Coming Up** panel, but it's still visible. Why?

    Browsers read code from top to bottom. The HTML for the **comingUpContent** element is down in the **<body>**. Because the JavaScript that references this object is at the top of the file (before the element has actually been created) our JavaScript code fails! To avoid this problem, it's a best practice to put JavaScript at the bottom of the HTML instead of at the top. This ensures all elements have been created before the JavaScript is executed.

15. Switch back to your code editor.

16. Cut the entire **<script>** tag (and its contents) from the head.

17. Paste it just above the closing **</body>** tag (around line 86):

```
</div>
<script>
   document.getElementById('comingUpContent').style.display = 'none';
</script>
</body>
```

Now that our JavaScript code comes after the **comingUpContent** element has been created, it should work.

18. Save the file, switch to the browser, and reload **index.html**.

19. Notice that the **Coming Up** panel's content is hidden. Now that it's in the proper place, our code is working!

    NOTE: Our code is not inside a function and so it is executed immediately when the page loads.

20. Switch back to your code editor.

21. Let's hide the **pastEventsContent** div using the same technique. Inside the **script** tag, add the following bold code:

```
<script>
   document.getElementById('comingUpContent').style.display = 'none';
   document.getElementById('pastEventsContent').style.display = 'none';
</script>
```

22. Save the file, switch to the browser, and reload **index.html**. The content for the **Coming Up** and **Past Events** panels should both be hidden.

## Hiding & Showing Content When the User Clicks

1. Switch back to your code editor.

2. Let's code the functionality to show the **Coming Up** panel. We don't want this to happen until we click on the panel's tab, so we must put this into a function. Add the following bold code:

```
   document.getElementById('comingUpContent').style.display = 'none';
   document.getElementById('pastEventsContent').style.display = 'none';

   function showComingUp() {

   }
</script>
```

3. Let's target the **comingUpContent** div and show it. Type the following bold code:

```
document.getElementById('comingUpContent').style.display = 'none';
document.getElementById('pastEventsContent').style.display = 'none';

function showComingUp() {
   document.getElementById('comingUpContent').style.display = 'block';
}
</script>
```

This statement says to get the element that has the ID **comingUpContent** and set its **display** property to **block**, which will make the div visible when the showComingUp() function is triggered.

4. Now that we have written the function, we need to call it when the user clicks the **Coming Up** tab. Around line 39, add the following bold code to the **comingUpTab** div:

```
<div class="accordionPanelTab" id="comingUpTab" onclick="showComingUp();">
Coming Up</div>
```

This will run the **showComingUp()** function we just created when the **comingUpTab** div is clicked.

5. Save the file, switch to the browser, and reload **index.html**.

6. Click the **Coming Up** tab. Notice that its content is shown.

This is good, but we also need to **hide** the other open panels. Because we will need to hide all the panels for every tab, we'll create a separate function that we can reuse.

7. Switch back to your code editor.

8. Make a function called **hidePanels()** that hides all of the content panels by adding the following bold code:

```
document.getElementById('comingUpContent').style.display = 'none';
document.getElementById('pastEventsContent').style.display = 'none';

function hidePanels() {
   document.getElementById('eventsWeekContent').style.display = 'none';
   document.getElementById('comingUpContent').style.display = 'none';
   document.getElementById('pastEventsContent').style.display = 'none';
}
function showComingUp() {
   document.getElementById('comingUpContent').style.display = 'block';
}
```

When the hidePanels() functions is triggered, all three content divs will have their **display** property set to **none**, which will make the divs invisible.

9. Now we need to set **hidePanels()** to run in the **showComingUp()** function. Add the following bold code:

```
function hidePanels() {
    ( CODE OMITTED TO SAVE SPACE )
}
function showComingUp() {
    hidePanels();
    document.getElementById('comingUpContent').style.display = 'block';
}
```

Now, when the **showComingUp()** function runs, it first hides all the open panels, then opens the **comingUpContent** div.

10. Save the file, switch to the browser, and reload **index.html**.

11. Click the **Coming Up** tab. The panel that's currently open gets closed and the **Coming Up** panel opens. The other tabs don't yet work though. Let's write functions for them next.

## Finishing the Other Panels

1. Switch back to your code editor.

2. Copy the **showComingUp()** function.

3. Paste a copy directly **above** it.

4. Change the following bold code:

```
function hidePanels() {
    ( CODE OMITTED TO SAVE SPACE )
}
function showEventsWeek() {
    hidePanels();
    document.getElementById('eventsWeekContent').style.display = 'block';
}
function showComingUp() {
```

5. Now that we have the **showEventsWeek()** function coded, we need to call it when the user clicks the **Events This Week** tab. Around line 26, add the bold code to the **eventsWeekTab** div to tell JavaScript to run the function when the div is clicked:

```
<div class="accordionPanelTab" id="eventsWeekTab"
onclick="showEventsWeek();">Events This Week</div>
```

6. Save the file, switch to the browser, and reload **index.html**.

7. Click the **Coming Up** tab, then click the **Events This Week** tab. Excellent, they are both working! Let's get the third tab working and we'll be done.

8. Switch back to your code editor.

9. Copy the **showComingUp()** function.

10. Paste a copy directly **below** it.

11. Change the following bold code:

```
function showComingUp() {
   hidePanels();
   document.getElementById('comingUpContent').style.display = 'block';
}
function showPastEvents() {
   hidePanels();
   document.getElementById('pastEventsContent').style.display = 'block';
}
</script>
```

12. Let's call the function when the user clicks the **Past Events** tab. Around line 52, add the following bold code to the **pastEventsTab** div so the function runs when the div is clicked:

```
<div class="accordionPanelTab" id="pastEventsTab"
onclick="showPastEvents();">Past Events</div>
```

13. Save the file, switch to the browser, and reload **index.html**.

14. Click all three events tabs to see the simple accordion works!

---

## Optional Bonus: Adding a Highlight to the Current Open Panel

It would be nice to highlight the panel that's currently open. We have already created a style for the highlight, we just need to add it with JavaScript.

1. Switch back to your code editor.

2. In the **css** folder, open **main.css**.

   Scroll down to the bottom and notice the **.highlight** rule we created. This changes the color and background-color of elements it is applied to. We'll use this rule to highlight the open panel's tab.

3. Return to **index.html** in your code editor.

4. Around line 26, find the **eventsWeekTab** element.

5. Notice that this element already has the **accordionPanelTab** class.

   Elements can have more than one class. We'll use use JavaScript to add the **highlight** class to this element when it's open.

6. Find the opening **script** tag (around line 86) and add the following code shown in bold. Make sure you add a **space** between the two class names so it reads: **'accordionPanelTab highlight'**

```
<script>
   document.getElementById('comingUpContent').style.display = 'none';
   document.getElementById('pastEventsContent').style.display = 'none';
   document.getElementById('eventsWeekTab').className = 'accordionPanelTab
highlight';
```

   NOTE: The **eventsWeekTab** element currently has the **accordionPanelTab** class, so we're adding **highlight** as a second class.

7. Save the file, switch to Chrome, and reload **index.html**.

8. Notice that the **Events This Week** tab is now highlighted with a lighter gray background and gold text.

9. Switch back to your code editor.

10. Let's use our existing functions to turn this highlighting on for the tab that's currently open, and turn it off for the other tabs. Add the following JavaScript shown in bold, remembering to add a space between the class names.

```
function showEventsWeek() {
   hidePanels();
   document.getElementById('eventsWeekContent').style.display = 'block';
   document.getElementById('eventsWeekTab').className = 'accordionPanelTab
highlight';
}
function showComingUp() {
   hidePanels();
   document.getElementById('comingUpContent').style.display = 'block';
   document.getElementById('comingUpTab').className = 'accordionPanelTab
highlight';
}
function showPastEvents() {
   hidePanels();
   document.getElementById('pastEventsContent').style.display = 'block';
   document.getElementById('pastEventsTab').className = 'accordionPanelTab
highlight';
}
```

11. Save the file, switch to Chrome, and reload **index.html**.

12. Click each of the tabs. The highlight gets applied, but it stays on. We need to also remove the highlights for the tabs that are not currently active.

13. Switch back to your code editor.

14. Find the **hidePanels()** function (around line 91).

15. We can add the code to remove all the highlights to this **hidePanels()** function. Remember that the hidePanels() function is triggered by the showEventsWeek(), showComingUp(), and showPastEvents() functions before they set their own highlight styles.

    Add the following bold code:

```
function hidePanels() {
    document.getElementById('eventsWeekContent').style.display = 'none';
    document.getElementById('comingUpContent').style.display = 'none';
    document.getElementById('pastEventsContent').style.display = 'none';
    document.getElementById('eventsWeekTab').className = 'accordionPanelTab';
    document.getElementById('comingUpTab').className = 'accordionPanelTab';
    document.getElementById('pastEventsTab').className = 'accordionPanelTab';
}
```

    NOTE: Highlighted panels have both the **accordionPanelTab** and **highlight** classes. Panels that are not highlighted should only have the **accordionPanelTab** class.

16. To recap what happens when a tab is clicked:

    • All panels are hidden.

    • All tabs have the highlight style removed.

    • The specific panel that was clicked opens and its associated tab gets highlighted.

17. Save the file, switch to Chrome, and reload **index.html**.

18. Click each of the tabs. Awesome, now it works with the highlight!

    NOTE: If you want to refer to our final code example, go to **Desktop > Class Files > yourname-JavaScript jQuery Class > Done-Files > Simple-Accordion**.

## Exercise Preview

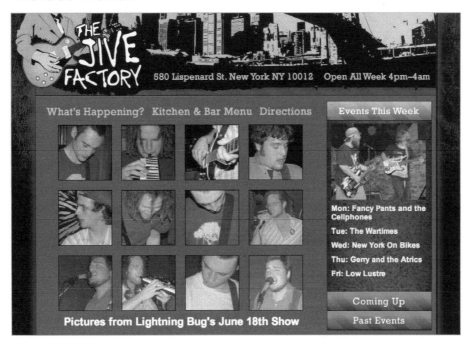

## Exercise Overview

In this exercise, we'll learn how to externalize JavaScript so it can be shared between pages.

---

## Getting Started

1. Open your code editor if it isn't already open.

2. Close any files you may have open.

3. For this exercise we'll be working with the **Sharing-JavaScript** folder located in **Desktop > Class Files > yourname-JavaScript jQuery Class**. You may want to open that folder in your code editor if it allows you to (like Sublime Text does).

4. Open **index.html** from the **Sharing-JavaScript** folder.

5. Preview the page in a browser. Notice on the right of this page, that there is the accordion you coded in the previous exercise. Test it out to see that it's working.

6. Switch back to your code editor.

7. Open **photo-gallery.html** from the **Sharing-JavaScript** folder.

8. Preview the page in a browser. Notice this page also has the accordion on the right, but it's not working because it doesn't have any JavaScript.

## Externalizing JavaScript

The photo gallery needs the same JavaScript code we currently have on the homepage (index.html). If we copy and paste the JavaScript code we'll end up with two copies, making later updates harder. As a better alternative, we'll move the JavaScript code into a shared JavaScript (.js) file, and link both HTML pages to it.

1. Switch back to your code editor.

2. Switch back to **index.html**.

3. Find the **script** tag around line 86.

4. Select all the code **between** the opening and closing **script** tags. Don't select the **<script>** and **</script>** tags!

```
<script>
    document.getElementById('comingUpContent').style.display = 'none';
      ( CODE OMITTED TO SAVE SPACE )


    function showEventsWeek() {
      ( CODE OMITTED TO SAVE SPACE )

    }
    function showComingUp() {
      ( CODE OMITTED TO SAVE SPACE )

    }
    function showPastEvents() {
      ( CODE OMITTED TO SAVE SPACE )

    }
    function hidePanels() {
      ( CODE OMITTED TO SAVE SPACE )

    }
</script>
```

5. Cut the code.

6. Create a new file.

7. Paste the code into it.

   TIP: If you're using Sublime Text, you can use **Edit > Paste and Indent** to keep the code indention looking nice.

8. Save the file as **main.js** into the **js** folder in the **Sharing-JavaScript** folder.

## Linking to the JavaScript File

We need to link our HTML file to the external JavaScript file we just made.

1. Switch back to **index.html**.

2. Scroll to the bottom and find the empty **script** tags around line 86.

3. Edit the tags as shown below (make sure to delete any extra lines and spaces between the opening and closing script tags):

   ```
   <script src="js/main.js"></script>
   ```

4. Save and preview the file. Test out the accordion to see it should still be working.

5. Switch back to your code editor.

6. Switch to **photo-gallery.html**.

7. At the bottom of the document, before the closing **</body>** tag add the following bold code:

   ```
   </div>
   <script src="js/main.js"></script>
   </body>
   ```

8. Save and preview the file in a browser. Test out the accordion to see it is now working on this page as well. Sweet.

   NOTE: If you want to refer to our final code example, go to **Desktop > Class Files > yourname-JavaScript jQuery Class > Done-Files > Sharing-JavaScript**.

---

### External JavaScript

It's a best practice to externalize JavaScript and you should always do so when you're ready to go live. For the sake of simplicity, however, we'll continue to write JavaScript inside our HTML documents for the next few exercises. Later in the course we'll work with external JavaScript.

# Introduction to Arrays & the Math Object

## Exercise Preview

## Exercise Overview

In this exercise, we will learn about arrays and how to create them. We'll also learn about Math objects and how to use them in conjunction with arrays to display the values we want.

---

## Getting Started

1. Open your code editor if it isn't already open.

2. Close any files you may have open.

3. For this exercise we'll be working with the **Random-Testimonial** folder located in **Desktop > Class Files > yourname-JavaScript jQuery Class**. You may want to open that folder in your code editor if it allows you to (like Sublime Text does).

4. Open **index.html** from the **Random-Testimonial** folder.

5. Preview **index.html** in Chrome (we'll be using its DevTools later).

6. Notice the testimonial **NAPS is by far the most significant cultural force of the decade. – New York Times**.

   We want to use JavaScript to randomly show a different testimonial each time the page is loaded. In order to accomplish this, we'll be using an array. Think of an **array** as a list. We can store multiple values in a single array. The array stores items in a numbered list, so we can access any specific value by referring to its number (index) within the list. While you typically number lists starting with 1 (then 2, 3, etc.), JavaScript arrays start with 0 (then 1, 2, etc).

## Creating an Array

1. Before we start working on this page, let's first learn the fundamentals about arrays by experimenting in the Console. We'll start by create an array. To open Chrome's Console, hit **Cmd–Opt–J** (Mac) or **Ctrl–Shift–J** (Windows).

2. In the Console, type the following but do not hit Return/Enter yet!

   ```
   var myArray = [];
   ```

   NOTE: The **[]** denotes an array in JavaScript.

---

**TIP: Adjusting the Console's Text Size**

You can adjust the size of the Console text as follows:

- Mac: **Cmd-Plus(+)** enlarges the text. **Cmd-Minus(-)** reduces the text. **Cmd-0** resets to the default size.

- Windows: **Ctrl-Plus(+)** enlarges the text. **Ctrl-Minus(-)** reduces the text. **Ctrl-0** resets to the default size.

---

3. So far our array is empty. Add some values to the array as shown in bold:

   ```
   var myArray = ['Madrid', 'Paris', 'London'];
   ```

4. Hit **Return** (Mac) or **Enter** (Windows) to apply it.

5. The Console will print **undefined**, which is something we are not concerned with now.

   NOTE: Why does it say undefined? Some things in JavaScript return a result when they are executed. Creating an array does not return a value, so the return is undefined. In this case we don't care about a returned value, so you can proceed to the next step.

6. Type **myArray;** and hit **Return** (Mac) or **Enter** (Windows).

7. You should see **["Madrid", "Paris", "London"]** print out in the Console.

8. How do we get a specific value from this array? To get the first value, type:

   ```
   myArray[0];
   ```

   NOTE: Remember that arrays are **zero-indexed**, which means they start numbering with 0.

9. Hit **Return** (Mac) or **Enter** (Windows) to apply it and the string **"Madrid"** will print.

10. To get the third value, type:

    **myArray[2];**

    TIP: You can hit your **Up Arrow** key to reload the previous Console command.

11. Hit **Return** (Mac) or **Enter** (Windows) and the string **"London"** will print.

---

## Editing an Array

1. To change a value in an array, type:

   **myArray[2] = 'Beijing';**

2. Hit **Return** (Mac) or **Enter** (Windows) and **"Beijing"** will print.

3. Arrays have a variety of methods and we want to test out some of the commonly-used methods. Type the following so we can look at these methods:

   **console.dir(myArray);**

   NOTE: **dir** displays an interactive list of an object's properties. It stands for directory, as in an informational directory.

4. Hit **Return** (Mac) or **Enter** (Windows).

5. Expand the array's list by clicking the **arrow** to the left of **Array[3]**.

6. Click the **arrow** next to **__proto__: Array[0]** to see the methods we can use. Let's try some of these.

7. What if we want to add a value to the array? To do this, type the following code:

   **myArray.push('New York');**

   NOTE: You can put any value you want to add in the parentheses. Here, we're adding the value "New York" to the array.

8. Hit **Return** (Mac) or **Enter** (Windows). It prints **4** to show how many values are in the array.

9. Type **myArray;** and hit **Return** (Mac) or **Enter** (Windows) and it will show the values in the array:

   ```
   ["Madrid", "Paris", "Beijing", "New York"]
   ```

10. Checking how many values are in an array is very useful when writing dynamic code. To test it out, type the following:

    **myArray.length;**

11. Hit **Return** (Mac) or **Enter** (Windows) and **4** will print.

12. Sometimes it's useful to sort an array. JavaScript arrays have a **sort()** method that will work here. To test it out, type the following:

    ```
    myArray.sort();
    ```

13. Hit **Return** (Mac) or **Enter** (Windows) and the Console should print the cities in alphabetical order:

    ```
    ["Beijing", "Madrid", "New York", "Paris"]
    ```

14. Leave **index.html** open in Chrome so we can come back to it later.

## Creating an Array of Testimonials

Now that we've seen a bit of what arrays can do, let's get to work on replacing the static testimonial on the page with an array of various press quotes.

1. Switch back to **index.html** in your code editor.

2. Start adding a new array before the closing **</body>** tag (on line 46):

   ```
   </footer>
   <script>
      var quotesArray = [];
   </script>
   </body>
   ```

3. Inside the [] brackets, add some quotes by adding the following bold code:

   ```
   <script>
      var quotesArray = [
         'first quote',
         'second quote',
         'third quote'
      ];
   </script>
   ```

   NOTE: Our values are strings, so each quote must be surrounded by single quotes. Note that each string is separated by a comma, but there's no comma after the last string.

4. Save the file.

5. Switch to **index.html** in Chrome and reload the page.

6. Open the Console if it's not already open.

7. Type **quotesArray;** and hit **Return** (Mac) or **Enter** (Windows). You'll see the quotes printed.

8. Now we need to figure out how to switch out the testimonial on the page. Go back to **index.html** in your code editor.

9. On line 32, notice that we've given the testimonial **p** tag an ID of **press-quote**.

10. Let's see if we can change the testimonial using the Console. Switch back to Chrome.

11. In the Console, let's grab the **press-quote** element:

    **document.getElementById('press-quote');**

12. Hit **Return** (Mac) or **Enter** (Windows) to apply it.

13. It should print the HTML element (the entire tag and it's contents). We only want the text inside the element though.

14. Hit your **Up Arrow** key to reload the previous command.

15. At the end, add **.textContent** so you end up with the following:

    document.getElementById('press-quote')**.textContent;**

16. Hit **Return** (Mac) or **Enter** (Windows) to apply it.

17. It should print the text string content:

    ```
    "NAPS is by far the most significant cultural force of the decade. — New York
    Times"
    ```

18. Let's try to change that text. Hit your **Up Arrow** key to reload the previous command.

19. At the end, add **= quotesArray[2]** so you end up with the following:

    document.getElementById('press-quote').textContent = **quotesArray[2];**

    NOTE: In this case, we're changing the text of the testimonial to the third quote in the array. Remember that JavaScript arrays start counting with 0!

20. Hit **Return** (Mac) or **Enter** (Windows) and notice the testimonial on the page now says **third quote**!

    Now that we know how to change the testimonial text, we need to find a way to choose a random testimonial.

---

## The Math Object

The **Math** object contains a lot of very helpful functions for doing various mathematical operations. Let's investigate to see if it can help us.

1. In the Console, type **Math;** and hit **Return** (Mac) or **Enter** (Windows).

2. Click the **arrow** next to **Math** (the Math object) to expand it. In it, you can see its properties and functions.

   The list starts off with constants (values that are not meant to be changed), such as **PI**. Constants are written in UPPERCASE. So for example, if you ever needed to do a mathematical operation that involves PI, type **Math.PI;** and it will give you the value of PI.

3. What we'll be focusing on right now is the **random()** method. Type:

```
Math.random();
```

4. Hit **Return** (Mac) or **Enter** (Windows). It'll print a random number between 0 and 1.

5. Hit the **Up Arrow** key to reload **Math.random();**.

6. Hit **Return** (Mac) or **Enter** (Windows) to see it generates a different random number.

   How can we apply this for our purposes? We can have JavaScript choose a random number within a certain range that we specify. Then we can use that number to choose an item from the quotes array. If we have five different testimonials, we'd tell it to pick a number between 0 and 4.

7. To get a random number between 0 and 4, type the following code:

```
Math.random() * 4;
```

   NOTE: This multiplies the random number by 4 so instead of getting a number between 0 and 1, it outputs one between 0 and 4.

8. Hit **Return** (Mac) or **Enter** (Windows) to see a random number between 0 and 4.

   One problem is that the number we get has many decimal places, but we need an integer (a whole number).

9. The **Math.floor()** method rounds **down** to the closest whole number. Type:

```
Math.floor(3.78);
```

10. Hit **Return** (Mac) or **Enter** (Windows) and it'll print out **3**.

11. The **Math.ceil()** function rounds **up** to the closest whole number. Type:

```
Math.ceil(3.78);
```

12. Hit **Return** (Mac) or **Enter** (Windows) and it'll print out **4**.

## Using the Math Object to Pick Random Testimonials

Now that we know how the **Math** object works, let's figure out how we can customize it for our purposes.

1. Switch back to your code editor.

2. First, let's add the actual press quotes to our array. We've saved you some time by typing out the quotes for you. Go into the **snippets** folder and open **press-quotes.txt**.

3. Select and copy all the text.

4. Close the file. If you aren't already in **index.html**, switch to it.

5. Select the three placeholder quotes.

6. Replace them by pasting the new quotes over them.

   NOTE: If you're using Sublime Text, you can paste with proper indentation by using **Cmd–Shift–V** (Mac) or **Ctrl–Shift–V** (Windows).

7. Save the file.

8. Switch back to Chrome, and reload **index.html**.

9. In the Console, type the following code but do not hit Return/Enter yet!

   ```
   Math.random() * quotesArray.length;
   ```

   This says to take a random number between 0 and 1 and multiply it by the **length** of the array. We could specify a certain number to multiply by (such as when we used 4 previously) but it's better to use a dynamic number. That way if the number of items in the array changes, you won't have to rewrite the JavaScript.

10. To round it down, wrap the line in a **Math.floor()** as shown below in bold (don't miss the end parenthesis):

    ```
    Math.floor(Math.random() * quotesArray.length);
    ```

11. Hit **Return** (Mac) or **Enter** (Windows) to apply the command. You should get a random integer between 0 and 4.

12. Hit the **Up Arrow** key and then hit **Return** (Mac) or **Enter** (Windows) to get another random integer.

13. Perfect! Now we can add this to our JavaScript. Select and copy the line you typed in the Console:

    ```
    Math.floor(Math.random() * quotesArray.length);
    ```

14. Switch back to **index.html** in your code editor.

15. In the **script** tag near the bottom of the document, make a new line below the array and paste the code, as shown in bold:

    ```
        ];
        Math.floor(Math.random() * quotesArray.length);
    </script>
    ```

16. To make this number easier to refer to, let's store it in a variable. Add the following code shown in bold:

    ```
    ];
    var randomNumber = Math.floor(Math.random() * quotesArray.length);
    </script>
    ```

17. Next we need to grab the testimonial that's currently on the page and replace it with a random one. Add the following bold code (as a single line of code):

    ```
    ];
    var randomNumber = Math.floor(Math.random() * quotesArray.length);
    document.getElementById('press-quote').textContent =
    quotesArray[randomNumber];
    </script>
    ```

18. Save the file.

19. Preview **index.html** in Chrome. (Reload if it's already open.)

    The page will randomly display one of the testimonials.

20. Reload the page a few more times to see a random testimonial each time. Cool!

    NOTE: We are leaving the static — **New York Times** quote in the HTML as a graceful fallback in case a visitor has JavaScript turned off (and for SEO purposes).

---

## Optional Bonus: Adding Quote Marks Around the Testimonial

The testimonial is looking good, but technically it contains both a testimonial and an attribution. It would be nice if the testimonial portion was surrounded by quotation marks. The testimonial and attribution are separated by an emdash. If you're not familiar with am emdash, it's longer than a typical hyphen. We can use JavaScript to split the string on that emdash, and then add quote marks to just the testimonial portion.

1. Switch back to **index.html** in your code editor.

2. The **split()** method will split a single string into an array of strings. We can specify the character (in this case an emdash) where we want to split the string. Let's test how split() works. Around line 57, add the following bold code:

    ```
    document.getElementById('press-quote').textContent =
    quotesArray[randomNumber];
    console.log( quotesArray[randomNumber].split('') );
    </script>
    ```

# Introduction to Arrays & the Math Object

3. Inside the single quotes of the split method, you'll need to type an **em dash (–)** as follows:

   • Mac: Hit **Shift–Opt–Hyphen(-)**

   • Windows: Hold **Alt** as you type **0151** (on the Keypad) and then release **Alt**. If it doesn't work, hit the **Num Lock** key and try again.

   You should end up with the following code:

   ```
   console.log( quotesArray[randomNumber].split('–') );
   ```

4. Save the file.

5. Switch to **index.html** in Chrome.

6. Reload the page.

7. Open the Console if it's not already open.

8. You'll see the new array of testimonial strings, such as the example below.

   ```
   ["NAPS has ushered in a new era of sleep. ", " USA Today"]
   ```

   Take note that split() has removed the emdash, and created two items in an array.

9. Expand the array's list by clicking the **arrow** on the left.

   We can see that this array has two values, the testimonial (index 0) and the attribution (index 1).

   You'll also notice a space at the end of the testimonial and at the beginning of the attribution. Because we only want to add quote marks at the testimonial, let's change how we're splitting the string to get a value containing just the testimonial.

10. Return to **index.html** in your code editor.

11. Add a **space** on both sides of the emdash so you end up with:

    ```
    console.log( quotesArray[randomNumber].split(' – ') );
    ```

    NOTE: Remember that spaces inside the quotes are the ones that matter.

12. Save the file and switch to **index.html** in Chrome (reload the page).

    Notice that now the two values are just text with no extra spaces.

13. Return to **index.html** in your code editor.

14. We want to add quotes to the testimonial (index 0), so add the following bold code:

    ```
    console.log( quotesArray[randomNumber].split(' – ')[0] );
    ```

15. Save the file.

16. Switch to **index.html** in Chrome and reload the page.

    Just the testimonial should show. Great! Now that we know our split is working, we can add it directly to our code.

17. Return to **index.html** in your code editor.

18. Select and copy **.split(' – ')[0]** from the console.log() line.

19. Paste it in the line above, as shown here:

    ```
    document.getElementById('press-quote').textContent =
    quotesArray[randomNumber].split(' – ')[0];
        console.log( quotesArray[randomNumber].split(' – ')[0] );
    </script>
    ```

20. We're done testing, so add double slashes // to comment out the **console.log()**:

    ```
    //console.log( quotesArray[randomNumber].split(' – ')[0] );
    ```

    NOTE: The Console is great for developers, but you should only use it during development. Once you've used it to test things, be sure to remove the code (or at least comment it out) so it does not execute on a live site.

21. Save the file.

22. Switch to **index.html** in Chrome and reload the page. Only the testimonial should be appearing on the page (it's now missing the emdash and attribution).

23. Return to your code editor.

24. Let's begin to add the quotation marks. After the equal sign, type **two single quotes**, and a **plus** (with spaces around it) as shown below in bold:

    ```
    document.getElementById('press-quote').textContent = '' +
    quotesArray[randomNumber].split(' – ')[0];
    ```

25. Inside the single quotes, type an **opening curly quote** as follows:

    - Mac: Hit **Opt–Left Bracket ([)**

    - Windows: Hold **Alt** as you type **0147** (on the Keypad) and then release **Alt**. If it doesn't work, hit the **Num Lock** key and try again.

    ```
    document.getElementById('press-quote').textContent = '"' +
    quotesArray[randomNumber].split(' – ')[0];
    ```

26. Save the file.

27. Switch to **index.html** in Chrome and reload the page. You should see an opening quote (") at the start of the testimonial on the page.

28. Return to your code editor.

29. Now let's add the closing quote. After the **.split(' — ')[0]** type a **plus** (with spaces around it), and **two single quotes** as shown below in bold:

    ```
    document.getElementById('press-quote').textContent = '"' +
    quotesArray[randomNumber].split(' — ')[0] + '';
    ```

30. Inside the single quotes, add an **closing curly quote** as follows:

    - Mac: Hit **Opt–Shift–Left Bracket ([)**

    - Windows: Hold **Alt** as you type **0148** (on the Keypad) and then release **Alt**.

    ```
    document.getElementById('press-quote').textContent = '"' +
    quotesArray[randomNumber].split(' — ')[0] + '"';
    ```

31. Save the file.

32. Switch to **index.html** in Chrome and reload the page.

    You should now have quotation marks to the start and end of the testimonial! We're still missing the attribution, so let's add it back in.

33. Return to your code editor.

34. To add the attribution (index 1), add the the bold code as shown below. Don't miss adding the **+** before the new code you're typing. (Feel free to copy and paste the first split and change 0 to 1.)

    ```
    document.getElementById('press-quote').textContent = '"'
    + quotesArray[randomNumber].split(' — ')[0] + '"' +
    quotesArray[randomNumber].split(' — ')[1];
    ```

35. Finally, we must add the emdash back in. As shown below, after the closing quote (") type an emdash with spaces around it. To type an emdash, use the following keystrokes:

    - Mac: Hit **Shift–Opt–Hyphen (-)**

    - Windows: Hold **Alt** as you type **0151** (on the Keypad) and then release **Alt**.

    ```
    document.getElementById('press-quote').textContent = '"' +
    quotesArray[randomNumber].split(' — ')[0] + '" — ' +
    quotesArray[randomNumber].split(' — ')[1];
    ```

36. Save the file.

37. Switch to **index.html** in Chrome and reload the page a few times. The testimonial should have quotes around it and the emdash and attribution should be back.

    NOTE: If you want to refer to our final code example, go to **Desktop > Class Files > yourname-JavaScript jQuery Class > Done-Files > Random-Testimonial**.

## Exercise Preview

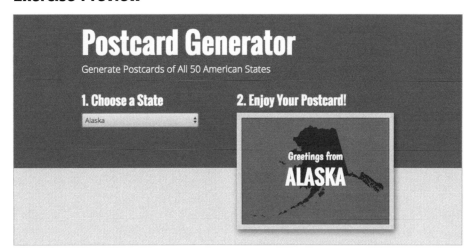

## Exercise Overview

In this exercise, you'll build a postcard generator. We'll have a single page where the user will choose from a list of U.S. states and the page will dynamically generate a postcard for that state. You'll learn about pulling values from a menu list, and use those values to change the text and image on the page.

---

## Getting Started

1. Open your code editor if it isn't already open.

2. Close any files you may have open.

3. For this exercise we'll be working with the **Postcard-Generator** folder located in **Desktop > Class Files > yourname-JavaScript jQuery Class**. You may want to open that folder in your code editor if it allows you to (like Sublime Text does).

4. Open **index.html** from the **Postcard-Generator** folder.

5. Preview **index.html** in Chrome (we'll be using its DevTools later).

   Notice the **Choose a State** menu on the left. When the user selects a state, we want to use JavaScript to generate a postcard with that state's name and a photo (showing the shape of the state).

6. Leave the page open in Chrome so we can come back to it later.

7. Let's take a look at the provided files. On your Desktop, navigate into **Class Files > yourname-JavaScript jQuery Class > Postcard-Generator** folder.

8. Open the **img** folder inside the **Postcard-Generator** folder.

   Within this folder there are 52 images: one for each of the 50 states, one for D.C., and one for the default "empty-state". We've named each state's image with the appropriate 2-letter abbreviation for that state.

9. Switch back to **index.html** in your code editor.

10. On line 21, find the **select** tag.

    The **select** tag creates the **Choose a State** menu. Notice it has an ID of **states**.

11. Within the **select** tag, notice there are **option** tags for each state.

    Each **option** tag has a **value** attribute, which we have assigned a 2-letter state abbreviation. These abbreviations match our corresponding image filenames. To generate the postcard, we will get the specific value from the option that the user chooses. We'll then use that value to know which image to display.

12. On line 78, locate the **div** tag with an ID of **postcard**. We'll be assigning the selected state's image (as a background-image) to this div.

13. On line 80, locate the **p** tag with an ID of **state-heading**. We'll be changing this text to the state's name.

---

## Getting Input From the Menu

Now that we have an idea of how the menu will work, we can use JavaScript to figure out which state the user has selected.

1. Add the following bold code before the closing **</body>** tag (around line 90):

```
</footer>
<script>

</script>
</body>
```

2. To make it easier to refer to the states select menu, let's store it in a variable. Type the following bold code:

```
<script>
   var states = document.getElementById('states');
</script>
```

3. When a user selects a new state from the menu, the menu fires an **onchange** event which we can listen for. We'll add a function that will only be triggered when the user selects a new state. Add the following code shown in bold:

```
var states = document.getElementById('states');
states.onchange = function() {

}
```

Unlike in previous exercises, notice that we are using an **onchange** event handler directly in JavaScript. This way we don't have to add it to the HTML.

Secondly, notice we did not give the function a name. These are called **anonymous functions**. Because it's a function, it will prevent the code we're going to put inside it from being executed right away. But we don't need to give this function a name, because it will be automatically executed when the states menu changes.

> **Unobtrusive JavaScript**
>
> Previously, whenever we wanted to trigger a function (when the user clicked on, focused on, or blurred off of an element), we'd add an event like **onclick** on the HTML element which calls a JavaScript function.
>
> **Unobtrusive JavaScript** is an approach that separates JavaScript and HTML code. By keeping all the JavaScript together, it's easier to find and edit.

4. The states menu contains all of the **option** values, which are also stored in an **options** array. We can figure out which **option** (state) the user selected from the menu, based on its position in the array (its "index").

   We can use **states.selectedIndex** to get the position (index) of the selected menu option within the array. Add the following bold code:

```
states.onchange = function() {
    console.log('state index: ' + states.selectedIndex);
}
```

5. Let's test this out. Save the file.

6. Preview **index.html** in Chrome.

7. Open Chrome's Console by hitting **Cmd–Opt–J** (Mac) or **Ctrl–Shift–J** (Windows).

8. Select **Alabama** from the menu.

   It should return **state index: 1**. Alabama has an index of 1 because the default "empty-state" (United States of America) is the first option (0) in the array.

9. Choose a different state to see that the Console returns a different index number for that selected state.

10. Return to **index.html** in your code editor.

11. Let's see if we can get a state's name. Add the following bold code:

```
states.onchange = function() {
    console.log('state index: ' + states.selectedIndex);
    console.log('state name: ' + states.options[0].text);
}
```

12. Save the file.

13. Switch to **index.html** in Chrome and reload the page.

14. From the menu, choose a state. Then choose a second state.

    Notice that the Console will show the appropriate **state index** of the selected state, but **state name** will always show **United States of America**. This is because we told the **options** array to only look for the first value (index 0).

15. Return to **index.html** in your code editor.

16. Instead of 0, let's feed **states.selectedIndex** into the **options[]** array so we'll get the name of the selected state. Add the following bold code:

```
states.onchange = function() {
    console.log('state index: ' + states.selectedIndex);
    console.log('state name: ' + states.options[states.selectedIndex].text);
}
```

17. Save the file, switch to Chrome, and reload the page.

18. Choose a state from the menu. The Console now returns both the appropriate **state index** and **state name**. Now we know how to get the values we need, we can continue on!

19. Switch back to your code editor.

20. We also need an image for the postcard, so we'll get the path to the image for the selected state. Add the following bold code:

```
states.onchange = function() {
    console.log('state index: ' + states.selectedIndex);
    console.log('state name: ' + states.options[states.selectedIndex].text);
    console.log('img/' + states.value + '@2x.jpg');
}
```

21. Save the file, switch to Chrome, and reload the page.

22. Choose a state from the menu to see that the Console now also returns the image path to the corresponding image for the selected state. For example, if you choose **Alabama** you should see **img/al@2x.jpg** in the Console.

23. Switch back to your code editor.

24. Now that we know the image path works, let's use it to change the background-image of the **postcard** element. Add the following bold code (keep it on one line):

```
states.onchange = function() {
    console.log('state index: ' + states.selectedIndex);
    console.log('state name: ' + states.options[states.selectedIndex].text);
    console.log('img/' + states.value + '@2x.jpg');
    document.getElementById('postcard').style.backgroundImage = 'url(img/' +
states.value + '@2x.jpg)';
}
```

25. Save the file, switch to Chrome, and reload the page.

26. Choose a few states, and notice on the postcard, that the background image behind **Choose a State** should change to the state you selected.

27. Switch back to your code editor.

28. We want the name of the selected state to appear on the postcard. We've already seen how to get the value from the selected menu option, so now we can use this to change the **state-heading** text. Add the following bold code (keep it on one line):

```
    document.getElementById('postcard').style.backgroundImage = 'url(img/' +
states.value + '.jpg)';
    document.getElementById('state-heading').innerHTML =
states.options[states.selectedIndex].text;
}
```

NOTE: We use **innerHTML** to refer to the contents inside an HTML element.

29. Save the file, switch to Chrome, and reload the page.

30. Choose a few states, and notice on the postcard, that **Choose a State** should change to the name of the state you selected.

31. Switch back to your code editor.

32. Finally, we'll finish off the postcard by changing the **greeting** element's text to **Greetings from**. Add the following bold code:

```
document.getElementById('postcard').style.backgroundImage = 'url(img/' +
states.value + '.jpg)';
document.getElementById('greeting').innerHTML = 'Greetings from';
document.getElementById('state-heading').innerHTML =
states.options[states.selectedIndex].text;
```

33. Save the file, switch to Chrome, and reload the page.

34. Choose a state, and notice that **To Generate a Postcard** should change to **Greetings from**.

Everything should be working now. Every time you choose a state, a complete postcard should be generated.

35. Switch back to your code editor.

36. We're done testing, so comment out the three **console.log()** lines by adding **//** to the beginning of each line.

    TIP: In Sublime Text you can select the lines and hit **Cmd–/** (Mac) or **Ctrl–/** (Windows) to comment them out.

    NOTE: When you're done troubleshooting, it's a best practice to either delete the Console code or comment it out.

37. Save the file.

    NOTE: If you want to refer to our final code example, go to **Desktop > Class Files > yourname-JavaScript jQuery Class > Done-Files > Postcard-Generator**.

    _____

# Introduction to JavaScript Objects & the DOM

## Exercise Preview

## Exercise Overview

JavaScript is called an **object-oriented language** because nearly everything in JavaScript is an **object**. An **object** is a collection of properties. Each property is a name (**key**) with a value, which are often called **key-value** pairs. If an object's property value is a function, we'd call it a method.

Objects can store many properties, so they can represent complex, real-world things. For example, a car object might include such properties as doors, color, seats, etc.

In this exercise you'll learn the basics about JavaScript objects. You will create your own object and learn how to access objects inside an HTML document to see how you can manipulate them.

## Getting Started

1. Open your code editor if it isn't already open.

2. Close any files you may have open.

3. In your code editor, hit **Cmd–O** (Mac) or **Ctrl–O** (Windows) to open a file.

4. Navigate to the **Desktop** and go into the **Class Files** folder, then **yourname-JavaScript jQuery Class** folder, then **Objects**.

5. Double–click on **js-objects.html** to open it.

   This is a basic page with some styles and an h1 heading with an ID of **main-heading**.

6. Preview **js-objects.html** in Chrome. (We'll be using its DevTools later.)

   All you'll see is the heading on a gray background. We will be creating our own object and taking a look at objects that are native to the browser.

7. Leave the page open in Chrome so we can come back to it later.

## Intro to Objects

1. Switch back to your code editor.

2. On line 19, add the **script** tags shown in bold:

```
<h1 id="main-heading">Introduction to JavaScript Objects</h1>
<script>

</script>
</body>
```

3. Now create a variable where we'll save our object:

```
<script>
   var myObject = {};
</script>
```

NOTE: **myObject** is the name of our object. You can name an object anything as long as it doesn't start with a number. The **{}** denotes an object in JavaScript.

4. Inside the object, add the following code shown in bold:

```
var myObject = {
   name: 'Bob'
};
```

NOTE: myObject now contains a single property called **name** that has the string value **Bob**. Properties can be named anything you like (as long as it starts with a lowercase letter). Properties can also be assigned values of any type (e.g. string, number, boolean etc.). For example, we could set up a **married** property for myObject and give it the Boolean value **false**. Properties and their values are often referred to as **key-value pairs**, where **name** is the **key** and **Bob** is the **value**.

5. Save the file.

6. Go back to **js-objects.html** in Chrome and reload the page.

7. Open Chrome's Console by hitting **Cmd–Opt–J** (Mac) or **Ctrl–Shift–J** (Windows).

8. In the Console, type **myObject;** then hit **Return** (Mac) or **Enter** (Windows).

   You should see the Console print out: **Object {name: "Bob"}**

9. Let's try using dot syntax to see if we can access the object's **name** property. Type the following:

   **myObject.name;**

10. Hit **Return** (Mac) or **Enter** (Windows). Success! The Console prints out only the value of name: **"Bob"**.

11. Switch back to your code editor.

12. As shown below, add a key with a number value. Multiple key-value pairs in an object are separated by commas, so make sure not to miss the **comma** after **'Bob'**:

```
<h1 id="main-heading">Introduction to JavaScript Objects</h1>
<script>
    var myObject = {
        name: 'Bob',
        age: 23
    };
</script>
```

NOTE: The additional values don't need to start on a new line but it can help make the code look a little neater and easier to read.

13. Add another key-value pair, this time with a Boolean value:

```
<script>
    var myObject = {
        name: 'Bob',
        age: 23,
        alive: true
    };
</script>
```

NOTE: A boolean value can only either be **true** or **false**.

14. Save the file.

15. Reload **js-objects.html** in Chrome.

16. The Console should still be open but if you closed it, hit **Cmd–Opt–J** (Mac) or **Ctrl–Shift–J** (Windows) to open it.

17. In the Console, type **myObject;** then hit **Return** (Mac) or **Enter** (Windows).

    The Console should print everything in the object (name, age, and alive).

18. Let's check Bob's vitals by looking at just the **alive** value. Type **myObject.alive;** then hit **Return** (Mac) or **Enter** (Windows).

    Phew, it should print out the boolean value **true**.

19. Let's add another key-value pair dynamically here in the Console. For example, let's say we want to add a hair color value for Bob. Type:

    **myObject.hairColor = 'brown';**

    NOTE: Remember that any code you write directly to the Console in a browser is only for test purposes and will not be saved in your working document. Make sure not to reload the page, as you will lose your work!

20. Hit **Return** (Mac) or **Enter** (Windows) to apply it.

    The Console prints out: **"brown"**.

21. To check if this change has been added to our object, type **myObject.hairColor;** then hit **Return** (Mac) or **Enter** (Windows).

22. Type **myObject;** then hit **Return** (Mac) or **Enter** (Windows) to see all the object's properties, including the hairColor we just added.

23. Bob just had his birthday so we need to change his age. It's easy to change a value in the Console! Type the following then hit **Return** (Mac) or **Enter** (Windows).

    ```
    myObject.age = 24;
    ```

24. Type **myObject;** then hit **Return** (Mac) or **Enter** (Windows) to see that the age property has been updated to **24**. Neat!

    NOTE: If you're working in Chrome and want to clear the Console's code without reloading the page and losing your work, hit **Cmd–K** (Mac) or **Ctrl–L** (Windows).

## The Global Object

All the properties have been added to the **global object** (also known as the **window** in the browser environment). The global object/window is literally the browser window. It is the furthest out you can go in front-end development.

1. Let's look inside the global object. In the Console, type **console.dir(window);** then hit **Return** (Mac) or **Enter** (Windows).

2. Click the **arrow** to the left of **Window** to expand it.

3. We're looking for a property that starts with lowercase. These are listed below the ones that begin with uppercase. Scroll down until you find **myObject: Object**.

4. When you find it, click the **arrow** to the left of **myObject: Object** to expand it and see the properties we've specified.

   With JavaScript, you can see everything inside this object as well as the objects inside this object. You may have been wondering, while working on previous exercises, where we can find all the methods and properties we need to manipulate elements on the webpage. Now we can see how to access all of this inside each object.

   We've included a handy diagram in your class files to help you get a better understanding of this.

5. Keep the page open in Chrome (with the Console open), and switch to your Desktop.

6. On the **Desktop**, go into **Class Files > yourname-JavaScript jQuery Class > Objects** and open **dom.pdf**.

   This shows a simplified version of the structure of the **window** object (showing just a few example objects). First off, everything is contained inside the topmost node, the **window/global object**. Think of the window object as the browser window. Within the window object, notice the **document**. This is where all HTML elements live and where you'll spend most of your time when you're working in JavaScript.

7. Notice that in addition to the **document** object, we also have access to the **location** object.

8. Keep **dom.pdf** open so you can refer back to it later.

9. Switch back to Chrome.

10. You should still have the Console open with the Window object still expanded. If you don't have the Console open:

    • Open the Console, type **console.dir(window);** and then hit **Return** (Mac) or **Enter** (Windows).

    • Click the **arrow** to the left of **Window** to expand it.

11. We're looking for a property that starts with lowercase again (below the uppercase properties at the top). Scroll until you find **location: Location**.

12. Click the **arrow** to the left of **location: Location** to expand it.

13. Locate **href** and notice that it shows us the file path of the webpage. In this case it's a local file path, but for a live site this would start with http.

14. Let's access this property of the window object. Type the following into Console:

    **window.location.href;**

15. Hit **Return** (Mac) or **Enter** (Windows).

    You should see the location (a file path) of the webpage.

16. The **location** property belongs to the **window** object, but because **window** is the global object and you can't go back any further than that, we don't ever have to type in **window** because it's already implied.

    Into the Console type **location.href;**

17. Hit **Return** (Mac) or **Enter** (Windows).

18. Notice that it returns the same value, even though we omitted the **window** object.

    NOTE: As another example, **alert()** also belongs to the **window** object. Because the **window** object is implied, both **window.alert();** or **alert();** will work.

19. Refer back to **dom.pdf**. Notice there are other objects listed under the window object:

    • The **history** object stores the locations of pages you've visited previously within a browser window.

    • We've already seen how to use the **console** object to output text to the Console.

---

## HTML Elements are Objects Too

Just about everything in JavaScript is an object. JavaScript treats HTML elements as objects. Previously, we've seen that we can use **getElementById()** to grab an element. That element is an object in JavaScript, which has properties that we can get and set.

1. Let's find an element on the page. Switch back to Chrome.

2. In the Devtools window, click the **Elements** tab.

3. Expand the **<body>** element and notice that the **<h1>** has an ID of **main-heading**.

4. Click on the **Console** tab.

5. We're going to want to refer to this h1 element numerous times, so let's store it in a variable to make it easier to reference. In the Console, type the following:

   ```
   var heading = document.getElementById('main-heading');
   ```

6. Hit **Return** (Mac) or **Enter** (Windows).

7. Type **heading;** then hit **Return** (Mac) or **Enter** (Windows).

8. The Console will print the HTML code for that element.

9. Let's break open this object and see what's inside it. Type the following then hit **Return** (Mac) or **Enter** (Windows):

   ```
   console.dir(heading);
   ```

10. Expand into **h1#main-heading**.

11. One property that we use a lot is the **style** property. Expand **style: CSSStyleDeclaration**.

12. The **style** property is another object that contains even more objects/properties (most of which are currently empty). Let's say we want to change the color. Type:

   ```
   heading.style.color = 'green';
   ```

   NOTE: You can specify a hexadecimal or RGB value as well.

13. Hit **Return** (Mac) or **Enter** (Windows) and notice that the heading has turned green (because we dynamically set it with JavaScript).

14. Let's also change the actual content of the text. Type the following code, then hit **Return** (Mac) or **Enter** (Windows):

    ```
    console.dir(heading);
    ```

15. Expand into **h1#main-heading**.

16. Scroll down to **innerHTML**. (If you see **(...)** click it to show more.) Take a look at the content.

17. Scroll down further to **textContent** to see what's there as well.

    Both innerHTML and textContent have the same content right now because there's no other HTML inside the heading. If we had any tags inside the h1, we'd see them listed in **innerHTML**. **textContent** only shows the text inside that element.

    If we wanted to edit the HTML content, we'd use innerHTML. If we just wanted to change the text, we'd use textContent.

    NOTE: You may have noticed that just below innerHTML was another property called **innerText**. innerText is a non-standard, proprietary property introduced by Internet Explorer and later adopted by WebKit/Blink (Safari/Chrome) and Opera. It can also be used to change text-based content, but because it is non-standard and not supported by Firefox, we recommend using textContent instead.

18. Let's test out the **textContent** property by changing the text. Type the following:

    ```
    heading.textContent = 'Hello';
    ```

19. Hit **Return** (Mac) or **Enter** (Windows) and notice the title change.

20. Let's test out the **innerHTML** property by adding an HTML tag. Type:

    ```
    heading.innerHTML = 'Hello, <em>world!</em>';
    ```

21. Hit **Return** (Mac) or **Enter** (Windows).

22. To see what the JavaScript did to our markup, switch to the **Elements** tab.

23. Expand the **<body>** element, then expand **<h1 id="main-heading" style="color: green;">**.

24. Notice the **<em>** tags have been added around **world!**.

    NOTE: If you want to refer to our final code example, go to **Desktop > Class Files > yourname-JavaScript jQuery Class > Done-Files > Objects**.

## Exercise Preview

## Exercise Overview

In this exercise, you will use JavaScript objects to dynamically update content without having to reload the page. In other words, we'll have a single page where when the user makes a selection, the information on the page will update without having to reload.

## Getting Started

1. Open your code editor if it isn't already open.

2. Close any files you may have open.

3. For this exercise we'll be working with the **State-Facts** folder located in **Desktop > Class Files > yourname-JavaScript jQuery Class**. You may want to open that folder in your code editor if it allows you to (like Sublime Text does).

4. Open **index.html** from the **State-Facts** folder.

5. Preview **index.html** in Chrome. (We'll be using its DevTools later.)

   What we want to do is create a finished webpage where the user can click on the **Choose a State** menu at the top right, choose a state, and see the info for it (without loading a new page).

6. Leave the page open in Chrome so we can come back to it later.

## Checking the Functionality of the Select Menu

1. Return to **index.html** in your code editor.

2. On line 16, find the **select** tag which contains the menu. Notice there is an **option** with a **value** attribute for each state. We will get the value from the option the user has chosen and we'll use that value to access stored data for each state.

3. Before we do that, we should take a look at the select menu in Chrome's Console to check that it's working the way we think it is. Switch to Chrome.

   You should still have **index.html** open.

4. Open the Console by hitting **Cmd–Opt–J** (Mac) or **Ctrl–Shift–J** (Windows).

5. It will be a good idea to save the state list select menu to a variable so we can access it more easily. In the Console, type:

   ```
   var stateList = document.getElementById('state-list');
   ```

6. Hit **Return** (Mac) or **Enter** (Windows).

7. To ensure it worked, type **stateList;** and hit **Return** (Mac) or **Enter** (Windows).

8. In the Console, the select menu will appear. Click the **arrow** to the left of the code to expand it and notice all the options.

   NOTE: If you'd like to clear the Console before continuing, hit **Cmd–K** (Mac) or **Ctrl–L** (Windows).

9. Back in the Console add the bold code shown below. Use **Shift–Return** (Mac) or **Shift–Enter** (Windows) to get to the next line without running the JavaScript.

   ```
   stateList.onchange = function() {
       console.log('changed!');
   };
   ```

10. Hit **Return** (Mac) or **Enter** (Windows) to apply it.

11. Test it out by going to the state menu on the page and choosing a state.

    In the Console you should see **changed!** appear. Each time you choose a state from the menu, the number beside **changed!** will increase to indicate how many times the message was logged.

12. Return to **index.html** in your code editor.

13. Add the following bold code before the closing **</body>** tag (around line 92):

    ```
        </div>
        <script>
            document.getElementById('state-list').onchange = function() {

            };
        </script>
    </body>
    ```

14. Save the file.

## Getting the Chosen Value

Now we want to get the value that the user chose. Let's figure out how to do that.

1. Switch back to Chrome but **do not reload** index.html.

2. In the Console, type the following and then hit **Return** (Mac) or **Enter** (Windows):

   ```
   console.dir(stateList);
   ```

3. Click the **arrow** next to **select#state-list** to expand it.

4. Scroll down to find **value**. That's what we need to get.

   NOTE: The **value** will be a 2-letter abbreviation of whichever state you chose, such as value="ak" or value="nj".

5. Return to **index.html** in your code editor.

6. Around line 94, type the bold test code shown below:

   ```
   <script>
      document.getElementById('state-list').onchange = function() {
          console.log(value);
      };
   </script>
   ```

7. Save the file.

8. Switch back to Chrome and reload **index.html**.

9. Choose a state from the menu. Oh no, we get an error: **Uncaught ReferenceError: value is not defined**.

10. Switch back to your code editor. The problem is that when we added **value** within **console.log()**, the browser assumes it is referring to the global object/window, which is not what we want. We need to specify that we want to get the **state-list**'s value.

    There are a couple of different ways to accomplish this. You could once again write `document.getElementById('state-list').value;` but that's really verbose and unnecessary.

    Instead, we can say we want to get the value of the object we're currently working in. JavaScript has a keyword called **this** which we can use. We could try to write `console.log(this.value);` but then the browser would assume **this** refers to the Console. Instead, let's assign **this** to a variable so we can be sure that we're working with **state-list**.

11. Add the following code in bold:

```
document.getElementById('state-list').onchange = function() {
   var selected = this.value;
   console.log(value);
};
```

12. Edit the code to use the **selected** variable to easily target the state-list:

```
document.getElementById('state-list').onchange = function() {
   var selected = this.value;
   console.log(selected);
};
```

13. Save the file.

14. Go to Chrome and reload **index.html**.

15. Choose a few states from the menu. You should see the abbreviation for each state you chose appear in the Console. Great!

---

**The JavaScript Keyword This**

In JavaScript, we use the keyword **this** much the way we use the demonstrative "this" in everyday natural language. Demonstratives like "this," "these," or "those" are used to show the relative distance between the speaker and the noun. As a result—in JavaScript, as in natural language—you must be careful to think about how "this" is determined. In the global context (outside of any function), **this** refers to the global object but an event property like onchange or onclick is owned by the HTML element it belongs to, therefore in that context **this** refers to the HTML element.

You can learn more about the JavaScript keyword **this** at tinyurl.com/javascript-keyword-this

---

## Dynamically Changing the State Name Value

In an earlier exercise we used the **value** and **textContent** of an **option** tag to make changes to an image and some text on screen. In that exercise we were limited in the amount of data that we could retrieve (an option element only has two pieces of data that we can use). In this exercise, we'll refer to an object that stores lots more information about each state. Now when our user chooses a state, we'll provide them with much more information than we were able to before.

Let's take a look at the object we'll pull our data from.

1. In your code editor, go into **State-Facts > js** and open **state-data.js**.

   In this huge file, we've declared an object that we can access by referencing the variable **stateData**. As you can see on line 1, the variable's value is wrapped in **{}**, which indicates that the value is an object.

   Inside the object are the state abbreviations, which are also objects that hold more key-value pairs for us to access. Once we call the state abbreviation, we can refer to the name of the property we need, such as **name**, **abbr**, **capitol**, etc.

2. In your code editor, switch back to **index.html**.

3. Let's start by changing the name under the map image. Around line 76, find the **info-name** paragraph. Let's set this to whichever state the user chooses.

4. Above the <script> tag, around line 92, link to the **stateData** JavaScript file as shown in bold:

   ```
   </div>
   <script src="js/state-data.js"></script>
   <script>
   ```

   NOTE: We now have access to everything in the stateData object! Let's take a look around our new object.

5. Around line 96, change the code to log our new **stateData** object, as shown below in bold:

   ```
   document.getElementById('state-list').onchange = function() {
      var selected = this.value;
      console.log(stateData);
   };
   ```

6. Save the file, switch to Chrome, and reload **index.html**.

7. Choose a state from the menu. In the Console you should see something like this:

   ```
   Object {usa: Object, al: Object, ak: Object, az: Object, ar: Object…}
   ```

   Any time we choose a state from the menu, the browser gives us the whole stateData object. While this demonstrates that we've successfully pulled in the stateData object, we need to narrow this selection to just the state we've chosen.

8. Back in your code editor, add the following bold code:

   ```
   document.getElementById('state-list').onchange = function() {
      var selected = this.value;
      console.log(stateData[selected]);
   };
   ```

9. Save the file, switch to Chrome, and reload **index.html**.

10. Choose a state from the menu. You should see something like this (depending on the state you chose):

```
Object {name: "Kansas", abbr: "KS", capitol: "Topeka", pop: "3,090,416",
statehood: "1861"…}
```

We're making progress. When we choose a state from the menu, we're grabbing all of the data from the corresponding state in the stateData object.

NOTE: The stateData object is a collection of states. We're accessing one state at a time by calling **stateData[selected]**. We used this syntax with arrays earlier, where we grabbed all the elements of an array (myArray) and then grabbed just a single element from the array (myArray[0]).

11. We're still grabbing too much data. We'd like to get just the name, or just the capitol of a given state, rather than all of the state's data. Let's narrow our selection down a little further.

Back in your code editor, add the following bold code:

```
document.getElementById('state-list').onchange = function() {
    var selected = this.value;
    console.log(stateData[selected].name);
};
```

12. Save the file, switch to Chrome, and reload **index.html**.

13. Choose a few states from the menu.

14. In the Console, you should see the name of each state you selected. Excellent! Now let's do something with our data.

15. Return to your code editor.

16. Delete the **console.log()** part of the line, including the end parenthesis so you end up with the following:

```
document.getElementById('state-list').onchange = function() {
    var selected = this.value;
    stateData[selected].name;
};
```

17. Set the **info-name** paragraph to use that text by adding the following bold code:

```
document.getElementById('state-list').onchange = function() {
    var selected = this.value;
    document.getElementById('info-name').textContent = stateData[selected].name;
};
```

18. Save the file.

19. Switch back to Chrome and reload **index.html**.

20. Choose a state from the menu and notice the state name below the map image changes. This name is the only thing that should change right now.

---

## Dynamically Changing the Rest of the Values

1. Switch back to your code editor.

2. The easiest way for us to set the other values is by copying/pasting the code we already wrote. Copy the following line (around line 96):

```
document.getElementById('info-name').textContent = stateData[selected].name;
```

3. Paste a copy as a new line, directly below.

4. The next value is the state abbreviation. Edit the code as shown:

```
document.getElementById('info-name').textContent = stateData[selected].name;
document.getElementById('info-abbreviation').textContent =
stateData[selected].abbr;
```

NOTE: In **state-data.js**, each state in the parent **stateData** object has a key named **abbr** that stores a value for the state abbreviation.

5. Save the file.

6. Switch back to Chrome and reload **index.html**.

7. Choose a state from the menu. Now you should see the state's abbreviation appear next to ABBREVIATION along with the state's name under the map image.

8. Return to your code editor.

9. Copy the **info-abbreviation** line (around line 97).

10. Paste it as a new line directly below.

11. As shown in bold, edit the pasted line of code so it will get the state capitol:

```
document.getElementById('info-name').textContent = stateData[selected].name;
document.getElementById('info-abbreviation').textContent =
stateData[selected].abbr;
document.getElementById('info-capitol').textContent =
stateData[selected].capitol;
```

NOTE: Remember you can find the **IDs** in **index.html** around line 75 (for the image) and lines 80–88 (for the other properties). The property names for the **stateData** object can be found in **state-data.js**.

12. Save the file, switch back to Chrome, and reload **index.html**.

13. Choose a state from the menu. Notice that the capitol also updates!

14. Switch back to your code editor.

15. Now that we can see how this works, we'll save some time by using some provided code. Go to **State-Facts > snippets** and open **change-function-code.txt**.

16. Copy all the code.

17. Close the file. If you aren't already in **index.html**, switch to it.

18. Select the three lines you already wrote.

19. Paste the new code over the three lines you already wrote.

    NOTE: If you're using Sublime Text, you can paste with proper indentation by using **Cmd–Shift–V** (Mac) or **Ctrl–Shift–V** (Windows).

20. Save the file, switch back to Chrome, and reload **index.html**.

21. Choose a state from the menu and you should see all the text info update. Yay!

22. The only thing left to change is the map image. To see where all the state images are stored, switch to the Desktop.

23. Go into the **state-facts** folder, then open the **img** folder to see all the state images. They have been conveniently named with the state abbreviations.

24. Switch back to **index.html** in your code editor.

25. Add the following bold code to get the state image to change:

    ```
    var selected = this.value;
    document.getElementById('info-pic').src = 'img/' + selected + '.jpg';
    document.getElementById('info-name').textContent = stateData[selected].name;
    ```

26. Save the file, switch back to Chrome, and reload **index.html**.

27. Choose a state from the menu and you should see the state image change, along with the rest of the info.

    Enjoy your dynamically updating State Facts page!

    NOTE: If you want to refer to our final code example, go to **Desktop > Class Files > yourname-JavaScript jQuery Class > Done-Files > State-Facts**.

---

## Exercise Preview

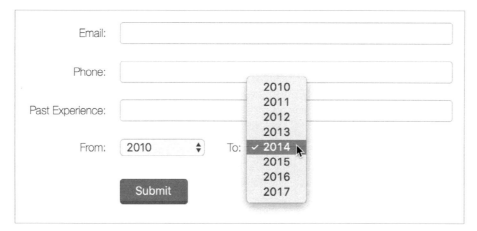

## Exercise Overview

One of the things that programming is really good for is repeating the same (or similar) actions very quickly. In this exercise, we'll look at one way to do this by using a **for loop**.

---

## Getting Started

1. Open your code editor if it isn't already open.

2. Close any files you may have open.

3. For this exercise we'll be working with the **Volunteer-Form** folder located in **Desktop > Class Files > yourname-JavaScript jQuery Class**. You may want to open that folder in your code editor if it allows you to (like Sublime Text does).

4. Open **index.html** from the **Volunteer-Form** folder.

5. Preview **index.html** in Chrome. (We'll be using its DevTools later.)

   This is a mockup of a form (which doesn't actually function). The only thing we're going to focus on are the From/To menus.

6. Click the menu next to **From**. Notice the range goes from **Before 2000** to **2017**.

   The **To** field is not selectable yet. We want to set it so that after choosing a From value, the To value only shows years equal to or later than the chosen From value.

7. Leave the page open in Chrome so we can come back to it later.

8. Return to **index.html** in your code editor.

9. Around line 36, locate the **select** tag with an ID of **from-year**. Notice that it contains **option** tags which we've already assigned values (years) to.

10. Around line 59, notice that the **select** tag with an ID of **to-year** is empty. For this **select** tag, we'll be generating the **option** elements using JavaScript.

## Creating a For Loop

Before we get further into this, we should take a look at what exactly loops are and how a for loop works.

1. Around line 66, add **script** tags as shown in bold:

```
</div>
<script>

</script>
</body>
```

2. Within the script tags, write a simple **for** loop by adding the following bold code:

```
<script>
    for() {

    }
</script>
```

The **()** are going to take three pieces of information. Inside the **{}** will be the instructions that we want to execute every time the loop runs.

3. Let's say we want to count from 0–10. First, we need to add a **counter** to count how many times it's going through the loop. Add the following bold code:

```
for(var i = 0;) {

}
```

We could name the variable anything but using **i** is a standard convention for incrementing. We also specified that the counter starts at **0**.

4. Every time the loop runs, it will check to see if a certain **condition** is true. If it is true, then we need to tell it what to do… inside the **{}**. If it's false, the loop will stop. Tell the loop to keep going as long as **i is less than 11** by specifying the condition:

```
for(var i = 0; i < 11;) {
```

5. Finally, we'll add the **incrementer** itself to specify that every time the loop runs, the value of i will increase by 1. Add:

```
for(var i = 0; i < 11; i++) {
```

NOTE: Alternately, you could write **i = i + 1** or **i += 1** to achieve the same results as **i++** (but with more characters).

6. Now we need to specify what happens each time the loop runs:

```
for(var i = 0; i < 11; i++) {
    console.log('The value of i is: ' + i);
}
```

7. Save the file.

8. Go back to Chrome and reload **index.html**.

9. If the Console isn't open, open it by hitting **Cmd–Opt–J** (Mac) or **Ctrl–Shift–J** (Windows).

10. Notice that the loop ran immediately upon page load and printed out the incrementing of i until it got to 10. Perfect!

---

## Using the For Loop to Set Menus

How will we use **for** loops in the volunteer application form? When the user chooses a year in the **From** menu, we want the **To** menu to show only the years between the selected year up to the current year (nothing earlier).

1. Switch back to **index.html** in your code editor.

2. Around line 67, **delete** the loop we wrote:

```
for(var i = 0; i < 11; i++) {
    console.log('The value of i is: ' + i);
}
```

3. We want to get the From and To field years and save them to variables. Type:

```
<script>
    var fromYear = document.getElementById('from-year');
    var toYear = document.getElementById('to-year');
</script>
```

4. We need to trigger an event whenever the user changes the **From** menu. For now, we want to check that it's working. Add the following bold code:

```
var fromYear = document.getElementById('from-year');
var toYear = document.getElementById('to-year');
fromYear.onchange = function() {
    console.log(fromYear.value);
};
```

NOTE: We're putting the **onchange** event handler directly in the JavaScript so we don't have to add it to the HTML.

5. Save the file.

6. Go back to Chrome and reload **index.html**.

7. Open the Console by hitting **Cmd–Opt–J** (Mac) or **Ctrl–Shift–J** (Windows).

8. Choose a year in the **From** menu. The Console should print out the year you chose, showing that it works.

9. Switch back to your code editor.

10. Start the loop around line 70, replacing the **console.log()** line:

```
fromYear.onchange = function() {
    for() {

    }
};
```

11. Start the counter with the following code:

```
for(var i = fromYear.value;) {

}
```

12. Add the condition that **i** should be less than or equal to **2017**:

```
for(var i = fromYear.value; i <= 2017;) {
```

13. Increase the value of **i** by 1 year:

```
for(var i = fromYear.value; i <= 2017; i++) {
```

14. Before we get any further, let's test our for loop. Add the following bold code:

```
for(var i = fromYear.value; i <= 2017; i++) {
    console.log(i);
}
```

15. Save the file, switch to Chrome, and reload **index.html**.

16. Open the Console if it isn't already.

17. Choose a year in the **From** menu.

    In the Console you should see a list of years from the year you selected up to 2017.

18. Choose a **different** year in the **From** menu.

    You should see a new list of years from the year you selected through 2017. The variable **i** is set to **fromYear.value**, the value you selected. Each time the loop runs, it tests to see if i is less than or equal to 2017. If it is, the loop runs. If not, the loop exits. Lastly, the i is incremented by 1 (i++) and the test is run again.

19. Switch back to your code editor.

   Now we need to add the years we generated into the **To** menu. So how are we going to create everything that goes into the **toYear** menu? Fortunately, JavaScript lets us assemble HTML elements, give them attributes, and put content inside them.

   For each year, we want to create an **option** element similar to the ones around lines 37–56. We want to create a new option every time the **for** loop runs, give the option a value, add text, then insert it into the **to-year** select tag. To do that we're going to need a variable that we can save everything in as we're assembling it.

   Around line 69, create the **option** variable by adding the bold code as shown below:

```
var toYear = document.getElementById('to-year');
var option;
fromYear.onchange = function() {
```

   NOTE: We're not assigning the variable to anything initially, which is fine.

20. Create the **option** element by replacing **console.log(i);** with the following code around line 72:

```
fromYear.onchange = function() {
   for(var i = fromYear.value; i <= 2017; i++) {
      option = document.createElement('option');
   }
```

   NOTE: **createElement()** is a method that belongs to the **document** object. You can put whatever element you want to create within the **( )**.

21. Set the **value** attribute to the selected year:

```
for(var i = fromYear.value; i <= 2017; i++) {
   option = document.createElement('option');
   option.setAttribute('value', i);
}
```

   NOTE: Within the **setAttribute()** method, **value** is the name of the attribute we want to set. We'll set **value** equal to **i**, which is the year currently in the loop.

22. Next, add the **textContent**:

```
for(var i = fromYear.value; i <= 2017; i++) {
   option = document.createElement('option');
   option.setAttribute('value', i);
   option.textContent = i;
}
```

   NOTE: In the previous step we set the **value** attribute of the option tag we're creating. In this step we're setting the content of that option element. If **i** is 2012, for example, we'll end up with something like this:

```
<option value="2012">2012</option>
```

23. Finally, we need a way to insert the option elements we're creating into the **to-year** select tag. Let's use the **appendChild()** method:

```
for(var i = fromYear.value; i <= 2017; i++) {
   option = document.createElement('option');
   option.setAttribute('value', i);
   option.textContent = i;
   toYear.appendChild(option);
}
```

NOTE: The **appendChild()** method adds a child element inside a parent element at the end of a list of any other child elements that may be present.

24. Save the file.

25. Switch to Chrome and reload **index.html**.

26. Choose a year in the **From** menu.

27. Click on the **To** menu and notice that it only lists years starting with the selected year through 2017.

28. Try setting a different **From** year.

29. Look in the **To** menu and notice it doesn't update appropriately. It keeps adding the next set of years to the end of the list without getting rid of the previous set.

## Clearing the To Menu

Fortunately, we can fix this pretty easily. Each time the loop runs, we want to clear out the **To** menu.

1. Switch back to your code editor.

2. Around line 71 add the following bold code. (Note that those are two single quotes!)

```
fromYear.onchange = function() {
   toYear.innerHTML = '';
   for(var i = fromYear.value; i <= 2017; i++) {
```

NOTE: We're using **innerHTML** rather than **textContent** because we need to change more than just the text.

3. Save the file.

4. Switch to Chrome and reload **index.html**.

5. Choose a year in the **From** menu.

6. Click on the **To** menu to make sure it only shows the years starting from your chosen year through 2017.

7. Choose another year in the **From** menu.

8. Click on the **To** menu again to see that it only shows the appropriate years. Great!

---

## Optional Bonus: Refining the Menu Selection Experience

What we've done so far works, but it's not the best user experience. For example, say the user has chosen a **From** and **To** date, but then needs to change just the **From** date again. When they do that, the **To** date will automatically reset, requiring them to set it again.

This functionality is acceptable only if the user accidentally chooses a starting year (From year) that is later than the end of their volunteer experience (the To year). In all other cases, we need to make sure the chosen To year stays constant. We'll remember the **To** menu's value by storing it in a variable. We can then use that saved value to reset the **To** menu after the **From** menu has changed.

1. Switch back to **index.html** in your code editor.

2. Around line 69, declare a variable for the value of the **To** year menu:

```
var option;
var toYearVal;
fromYear.onchange = function() {
```

3. Let's store the user's original **To** year value before we clear it out. Add the following bold code:

```
fromYear.onchange = function() {
    toYearVal = toYear.value;
    toYear.innerHTML = '';
```

4. After the loop is done running, let's first look to see if the **To** year value is greater than or equal to the starting point of the **From** year. Around line 79, add:

```
        toYear.appendChild(option);
    }
    if(toYearVal >= fromYear.value) {

    }
};
```

5. If the **To** year value is greater than or equal to the **From** year value, we want to make sure the original **To** year value remains unchanged. We can use the value we stored from the user's initial selection to make sure of that. Add the bold code shown below:

```
if(toYearVal >= fromYear.value) {
    toYear.value = toYearVal;
}
```

6. Save the file.

7. Reload **index.html** in Chrome.

8. Click on the **From** menu and choose a year.

9. Click on the **To** menu and choose a year.

10. Go into the **From** menu again and change it to an earlier year.

11. Notice the **To** menu should still have the same year you selected before.

12. Click on the **To** menu to see that the year range has been updated to start from the currently selected **From** year.

13. In the **From** menu, choose a year that is later than the current **To** year. You should see the **To** year update to the later year.

    NOTE: If you want to refer to our final code example, go to **Desktop > Class Files > yourname-JavaScript jQuery Class > Done-Files > Volunteer-Form**.

---

## Exercise Preview

## Exercise Overview

jQuery is an industry standard JavaScript library. They call it "The Write Less, Do More" library, which is 100% accurate. Other developers wrote a bunch of JavaScript code for you, and you just call their code instead of writing your own from scratch. It can be a huge time saver! In this exercise, you'll get started using jQuery by learning how to show and hide some content using a few different animations.

---

## Getting Started

1. Open your code editor if it isn't already open.

2. Close any files you may have open.

3. For this exercise we'll be working with the **Show-Hide-Basic** folder located in **Desktop > Class Files > yourname-JavaScript jQuery Class**. You may want to open that folder in your code editor if it allows you to (like Sublime Text does).

4. Open **index.html** from the **Show-Hide-Basic** folder.

5. Preview **index.html** in a browser.

6. Notice the **Contact** button in the top right.

   Something you can't see right now, is a **contact** div that contains the contact info (we've hidden it with CSS). When someone clicks the **Contact** button, we want to reveal the **contact** div using jQuery.

7. Leave the page open in the browser so we can come back to it later.

8. Return to **index.html** in your code editor.

9. Before we use jQuery, we must link to its JavaScript file. Find the closing **</body>** tag around line 70. Add the following bold code:

```
   </div>
   <script src="js/jquery-2.1.0.min.js"></script>
</body>
```

NOTE: Feel free to visit **jquery.com** to learn more about jQuery. Throughout these exercises we'll be linking our HTML to a downloaded version of jQuery we've provided for you. It's also possible to link to a version of jQuery stored online, an efficient way which you may choose to use in your own projects.

> **Minified vs. Regular Version**
>
> We linked to the minified version of jQuery. This compressed file is not human-readable, but it downloads faster. To see the difference, you can compare **jquery-2.1.0.min.js** and **jquery-2.1.0.js**.

10. This script file we just added gives us access to the jQuery library. Any jQuery we write will depend on this code and will have to be written **below** this `<script>` tag. Add the following bold code:

```
   <script src="js/jquery-2.1.0.min.js"></script>
   <script>

   </script>
</body>
```

## Using the jQuery Library

Query means to question. jQuery queries (searches) the DOM (Document Object Model) to find an element and then you can do something with it. You've seen how to use **getElementById()** to find an element with an ID, but what about classes, tags, etc? JavaScript also has a **querySelectorAll()** that can find elements using CSS selectors. jQuery is nearly the same: you pass the appropriate CSS selector to **jQuery()**. For example:

```
jQuery('#wrapper'); // select the element with an ID of 'wrapper'
jQuery('p');        // select all paragraphs on the page
jQuery('ul li');    // select list items inside unordered lists
jQuery('.special'); // select all elements with a class of 'special'
```

It would become pretty tiresome to type out **jQuery** over and over again. Since this is the "write less, do more" library, jQuery provides an alias for us to use: the dollar sign (**$**). The $ in the code we'll use going forward is just a shorter, more convenient name for the jQuery function.

## Running Code When the Document Is Ready

You always want the jQuery code to work as soon as possible. We've seen before that if JavaScript runs before the objects are ready, the code won't work. jQuery has dealt with this by creating a **ready** event that ensures nothing happens until the DOM is ready.

JavaScript has a similar event handler called **window.onload**, however jQuery's ready event, is speedier. While onload waits for all content to be loaded (for instance, images as well), jQuery's ready runs as soon as the objects are ready—the earliest time it can safely be run. This allows a user to start interacting with the script faster.

1. Add the following bold code:

```
<script>
    $(document).ready(function() {

    });
</script>
```

> ### TIP: Shortcut to Type $(document).ready() in Sublime Text
>
> 1. If you have the jQuery plugin installed in Sublime Text, typing this code is simple. Between the empty **script** tags type an **r** as shown below:
>
> ```
> <script>
>     r
> </script>
> ```
>
> 2. Select the **second** of three ready snippets **$(document).ready** and hit **Return** (Mac) or **Enter** (Windows). Voilà, it adds the code for you!

2. Save the file.

## Click Events

1. On line 13, locate **<a href="#" id="navContact">**.

   When the user clicks this button we want to show the contact info. We'll use jQuery to access this element, and make it clickable.

2. To select the element, add the following bold code:

```
$(document).ready(function() {
    $('#navContact')
});
```

jQuery uses the same selectors as CSS, so here we're selecting the element with the ID **navContact**.

3. In previous exercises we've seen how to write event handlers in JavaScript. jQuery also has event handlers. We want to track when the user clicks, so add the following bold code:

```
$(document).ready(function() {
    $('#navContact').click();
});
```

4. Now let's give it something to do. Inside the **click()** method's parentheses add the following bold code:

```
$(document).ready(function() {
    $('#navContact').click(function() {});
});
```

NOTE: jQuery will run the enclosed function whenever an element with the ID **navContact** is clicked. The **function()** is required by jQuery and surrounds the code so that it will only be executed on click.

5. Put the cursor inside the function's curly braces **{}** and hit **Return** (Mac) or **Enter** (Windows) to add an empty line, as show below:

```
$(document).ready(function() {
    $('#navContact').click(function() {

    });
});
```

NOTE: When you're working with jQuery and you see the series of characters **});** at the bottom of your function, you know you're on the right track.

6. Now we can add the code we want to **execute** when the Contact button is clicked. Add the following bold code:

```
$(document).ready(function() {
    $('#navContact').click(function() {
        alert('You clicked');
    });
});
```

NOTE: You can mix regular JavaScript with jQuery. Here we're using an **alert()**, just like we did earlier with plain JavaScript.

7. Save the file and reload **index.html** in Chrome.

8. Click on the **Contact** button to see the alert pop up that says **You clicked**.

9. Click **OK** to close the alert.

10. Switch back to your code editor.

## Showing & Hiding the Contact Info

1. Instead of the alert, let's make it reveal the contact info div (which we gave an ID of **contact**). Replace the **alert()** line with the following bold code:

```
$(document).ready(function() {
   $('#navContact').click(function() {
      $('#contact').show();
   });
});
```

Here we're using jQuery's **show()** method. There are hundreds of jQuery methods which you can browse at **api.jquery.com**

2. Save the file and reload **index.html** in Chrome.

3. Click on **Contact**. The **Contact Info** box should pop up. Looking good!

This a nice start, but we need to be able to close the contact info when we're done with it.

4. Switch back to your code editor.

5. Around line 21, find the **img** tag with the ID **closeBox**.

6. When the user clicks this button let's close the contact info (the **#contact** div). Add the following bold code:

```
$(document).ready(function() {
   $('#navContact').click(function() {
      $('#contact').show();
   });
   $('#closeBox').click(function() {
      $('#contact').hide();
   });
});
```

7. Save the file and reload **index.html** in Chrome.

8. Click on the **Contact** button. The **Contact Info** should appear.

9. Click on the **close** button (**X**) at the top right and the **Contact Info** should disappear. Nice!

10. Return to your code editor.

11. Let's try some other jQuery methods. Replace **show()** and **hide()** with the **toggle()** method, as shown in bold below:

```
$(document).ready(function() {
    $('#navContact').click(function() {
        $('#contact').toggle();
    });
    $('#closeBox').click(function() {
        $('#contact').toggle();
    });
});
```

12. Save the file and reload **index.html** in Chrome.

13. Click on the **Contact** button and notice the **Contact Info** still opens.

14. Click on **Contact** again. The **Contact Info** should disappear!

    The functionality is very similar, but now you can click the **Contact** button to both show and hide the **Contact Info**.

15. Switch back to your code editor.

16. Both the **Contact** and **close** buttons do the exact same thing now, so we can combine them together to simplify the code. Delete the **#closeBox** click() method shown below:

```
$('#closeBox').click(function() {
    $('#contact').toggle();
});
```

17. jQuery selectors can be written exactly the same as CSS selectors (with commas between each ID), so add the following bold code. Don't miss the comma!

```
$(document).ready(function() {
    $('#navContact, #closeBox').click(function() {
        $('#contact').toggle();
    });
});
```

18. Save the file.

19. Switch to the browser, reload **index.html**, and test it out. The **Contact** and **close** buttons should still work to open and close the **Contact Info**.

20. Return to your code editor.

21. Let's try out one more jQuery method. Replace **toggle()** with the following bold code (and don't miss the capital T in Toggle):

```
$(document).ready(function() {
    $('#navContact, #closeBox').click(function() {
        $('#contact').slideToggle();
    });
});
```

22. Save the file and reload **index.html** in Chrome.

23. Click on the **Contact** and **close** buttons to see the **Contact Info** now opens and closes with an animation. It's a nice effect that would have taken a lot more code if we'd written it in regular JavaScript.

NOTE: If you want to refer to our final code example, go to **Desktop > Class Files > yourname-JavaScript jQuery Class > Done-Files > Show-Hide-Basic**.

_____

## Exercise Preview

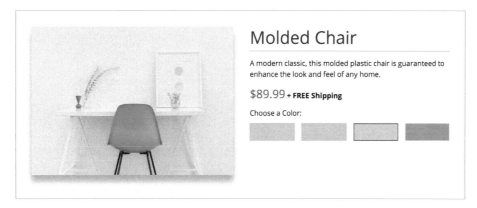

## Exercise Overview

When products are available in multiple colors, users need to be able to choose the color they want to receive. In this exercise, you will use jQuery to make a product color picker that lets a user choose a color and then see a photo of the product with the color they selected.

## Getting Started

1. Open your code editor if it isn't already open.

2. Close any files you may have open.

3. For this exercise we'll be working with the **Product-Color-Chooser** folder located in **Desktop > Class Files > yourname-JavaScript jQuery Class**. You may want to open that folder in your code editor if it allows you to (like Sublime Text does).

4. Open **product.html** from the **Product-Color-Chooser** folder.

5. Preview **product.html** in Chrome (we'll be using its DevTools later).

   Notice the large product photo showing the chair in one of its available colors. There are color swatches showing the other colors, but if you click on them they won't do anything yet. When a user clicks one of these color swatches, we want the photo to change to the color they clicked on.

6. Leave the page open in Chrome so we can come back to it later.

7. Switch back to your code editor.

8. Starting on line 21, notice that each of the four swatches have an **ID** for its color. We'll make use of those IDs later.

9. On line 29, notice there is an img with an **ID** of **product-photo**.

10. Notice the product-photo's source file is named **chair-beige@2x.jpg**. We have a total of 4 product images, which are named:

    - chair-beige@2x.jpg

    - chair-blue@2x.jpg

    - chair-red@2x.jpg

    - chair-yellow@2x.jpg

11. Notice that the color part of the image names listed above (**beige**, **blue**, **red**, and **yellow**), match the IDs we gave the swatch elements .

12. We're ready to code the JavaScript functionality. To use jQuery, we must link to its script file. On line 32, notice that we've already linked to jQuery for you (and an empty script tag below it for you write your JavaScript/jQuery code in).

13. To ensure that the jQuery code will not run until the document is ready, add jQuery's document ready code as shown below. Sublime Text Users can type **r** to bring up the **$(document).ready** snippet, then hit **Return** (Mac) or **Enter** (Windows):

```
<script)
    $(document).ready(function() {

    });
</script)
```

## Getting the Swatch Buttons to Work

1. When a user clicks one of the swatches we want to do something. Each of the swatches has a **swatch** class. Add the following bold code:

```
$(document).ready(function(){
    $('.swatch').click(function(){

    });
});
```

2. When a swatch is clicked we need to change the product photo by changing its **src** attribute to point to a different image path. We can change that attribute using jQuery's **attr()** method. jQuery's **attr()** takes two arguments: the attribute we're changing, and the value we're setting it to.

   Eventually we'll need to figure out which color image to show, but for now let's make sure we can change it to a different image. Add the following bold code:

```
$('.swatch').click(function(){
    $('#product-photo').attr('src', 'img/chair-blue@2x.jpg');
});
```

3. Save the file and reload the page in Chrome.

4. Currently the page is showing the beige chair. Click any color swatch and see that the photo changes to the blue chair.

   Now that we know we can change the image, we need to figure out which color the user clicked, and then show the appropriate photo.

## Figuring Out Which Color the User Clicked On

In an earlier exercise we learned that we can detect which element was just acted upon using JavaScript's keyword **this**. We can also use **this** in jQuery.

1. Switch back to your code editor.

2. On line 22, notice that we've given the yellow swatch an ID of **yellow**. If the user clicks on the yellow swatch, **$(this)** will refer to that element.

3. Near the bottom of the file, add the following bold code:

```
$('.swatch').click(function(){});
    $('#product-photo').attr('src', 'img/chair-blue@2x.jpg');
    console.log( $(this) );
});
```

4. Save the file and reload the page in Chrome.

5. Open the Console by hitting **Cmd–Opt–J** (Mac) or **Ctrl–Shift–J** (Windows).

6. Click on the **yellow** swatch and in the Console, notice that the whole element you clicked on is printed.

   We don't want the whole element, we just want the ID (to use when we build our image's file path).

7. Switch back to your code editor.

8. Add **.attr('id')** as shown below in bold:

```
$('.swatch').click(function(){
    $('#product-photo').attr('src', 'img/chair-blue@2x.jpg');
    console.log( $(this).attr('id') );
});
```

9. Save the file and reload the page in Chrome.

10. Click on the a few of the swatches and notice in the console that just the ID of the element you clicked on shows up in the console (**beige**, **blue**, **red**, or **yellow**).

11. Close the **DevTools** window.

12. Switch back to your code editor.

13. Instead of always switching the product photo to a specific image, we need to assemble the proper image path based on the color that was selected. In the file path **img/chair-blue@2x.jpg** only the color part (in this case **blue**) needs to change. Let's make that color part dynamic.

    On the **$('#product-photo')** line, inside the **.attr()** method, delete the **blue** and replace it with the following bold code:

    ```
    $('.swatch').click(function(){
        $('#product-photo').attr('src', 'img/chair-' + $(this).attr('id') +
    '@2x.jpg');
        console.log( $(this).attr('id') );
    });
    ```

14. Save the file and reload the page in Chrome.

15. Click each of the color swatches to see that they're working. The photo should change to the color you clicked on. Beautiful!

## Change the Border Color of the Selected Element

Currently the first swatch (beige) has a black border around it to indicate it is selected. When the user clicks on a different swatch we need to move the border to that color swatch so they know which color is selected. We've applied the border with a **selected** class.

1. Switch back to your code editor.

2. We no longer need the **console.log** line of code, so delete it.

3. jQuery has an **addClass()** method that does just what we want. Add the following bold code:

    ```
    $('.swatch').click(function(){
        $('#product-photo').attr('src', 'img/chair-' + $(this).attr('id') +
    '@2x.jpg');
        $(this).addClass('selected');
    });
    ```

4. Save the file and reload the page in Chrome.

5. Click the **red** swatch and its border color should change to black.

6. Click on the **blue** color swatch and notice that its border also changes to black, but the **red** and **beige** borders are still "stuck" on black. We need them to revert to their original border color. Let's fix that now.

7. Before we indicate which swatch gets the **selected** class, let's remove that class from all of the swatches. Add the following bold code:

```
$('.swatch').click(function(){
    $('#product-photo').attr('src', 'img/chair-' + $(this).attr('id') +
'@2x.jpg');
        $('.swatch').removeClass('selected');
        $(this).addClass('selected');
    });
```

8. Save the file and reload the page in Chrome.

   Click through all the color swatches and notice that only the one you click on should get the black border. The others will return to their original border color. Perfect!

---

## Using Hover Instead of Click

The product photo changes when the user clicks on a color swatch, but what if we wanted it to happen on hover?

1. Switch back to your code editor.

2. Change **click** to **hover** and shown in below in bold:

```
$('.swatch').hover(function(){
```

3. Save the file and reload the page in Chrome.

4. Mouse over the color swatches and notice the photo changes on hover. You no longer need to click.

   We're not saying this behavior is preferred, we just wanted to show you how to do both (and that it's easy to change).

   NOTE: If you want to refer to our final code example, go to **Desktop > Class Files > yourname-JavaScript jQuery Class > Done-Files > Product-Color-Chooser**.

---

## Exercise Preview

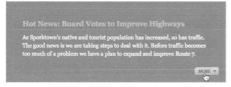

## Exercise Overview

In a previous exercise, you learned to show and hide content. In this exercise you'll take another look at showing and hiding, but with a new twist. You'll learn how to control the speed of jQuery's slideToggle() and learn more about targeting elements with jQuery.

## Getting Started

1. Open your code editor if it isn't already open.

2. Close any files you may have open.

3. For this exercise we'll be working with the **Show-Hide-Advanced** folder located in **Desktop > Class Files > yourname-JavaScript jQuery Class**. You may want to open that folder in your code editor if it allows you to (like Sublime Text does).

4. Open **history-news-jquery.html** from the **Show-Hide-Advanced** folder.

5. Preview the page in a browser to see what the page will look like to users.

   There is a div that contains the additional text and a button that will show/hide it. The additional text is hidden by default using the **.moreText** class. We'll use jQuery to add a cool animated transition to reveal the hidden content.

6. Leave the page open in the browser so we can come back to it later.

7. Return to your code editor.

   Before we use jQuery, we must link to its script file. Additionally, we are going to write our code in a main.js file. Before we code anything, we need to add these links.

8. Around line 91, add the following two links before the closing **</body>** tag:

```
    </div>
<script src="js/vendor/jquery-2.1.0.min.js"></script>
<script src="js/main.js"></script>
</body>
```

9. Save the file.

10. Go into the **js** folder and open **main.js**.

11. Add jQuery's document ready code. Sublime Text Users can type **r** to bring up the **$ (document).ready** snippet, then hit **Return** (Mac) or **Enter** (Windows):

```
$(document).ready(function() {

});
```

## Adding an Animation to Reveal Hidden Content

1. We want the text to be revealed whenever someone clicks the **More** buttons. All the **More** buttons have a **changeTextButton** class applied, so we'll use this to find out when they are clicked. Add the following bold code:

```
$(document).ready(function() {
    $('.changeTextButton').click(function() {

    });
});
```

This code tells jQuery to run the enclosed function whenever an element with the class **changeTextButton** is clicked. Remember that the **function()** is required by jQuery and surrounds the code that will be executed.

2. Each story has a div with a class style called **moreText** applied. The **moreText** divs are the hidden ones that we want to reveal. Inside that function, add the code shown below in bold:

```
$('.changeTextButton').click(function() {
    $('.moreText').slideToggle(500);
});
```

This says to do a jQuery **slideToggle()** animation to anything with the **moreText** class. The animation will last **500** milliseconds, which is half a second.

3. Save the file, switch back to the browser, and reload **history-news-jquery.html**.

4. Click one of the **More** buttons. Wow! They all expand (and collapse when clicked again). This is a good start.

## Targeting the Proper Div: Traversing the Document

Currently, the buttons affect all the divs simultaneously, but we only want to animate the div that holds the button we click. Fortunately, we can find the button that was clicked and use that to find the div.

1. Switch back to **main.js** in your code editor.

2. In the **click()** method, replace **'.moreText'** with **this** as shown below:

```
$('.changeTextButton').click(function() {
    $(this).slideToggle(500);
});
```

   Remember that **this** refers to the element or object that issued the event. We are clicking on the **More** button, so **this** refers to that clicked image.

3. Save the file, switch to the browser and preview **history-news-jquery.html**.

4. Click one of the **More** buttons to see the image slide away.

5. Switch back to your code editor.

6. Now that we see how to target the clicked image, let's find and target the **moreText** div in that same container. We've seen how JavaScript can maneuver around the document, and jQuery has the same concepts, but with more useful options. The following is a visual explanation of the concept of parent containers and siblings.

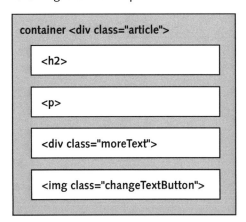

   The **.moreText** div and **.changeTextButton** img are both in the same container div. Because they are both in the same **parent** container, they are called **siblings**.

7. Add the **.siblings()** method as shown in bold. This will return all the elements that are in the same container (all the **children** of the same **parent**). The **More** button is sitting inside the container **article** div, so the image's siblings are all the other elements in that div.

```
$('.changeTextButton').click(function() {
    $(this).siblings().slideToggle(500);
});
```

8. Save the file.

9. Switch to the browser and reload **history-news-jquery.html**.

10. Click one of the **More** buttons to see that the **moreText** div slides open, but everything else in the container disappears. Not exactly what we're looking for, but we're getting close.

11. Switch back to your code editor.

12. We've successfully targeted all the elements in that container div, so the final step is narrowing it down to only the **moreText** div. Inside the parentheses of the siblings() method, add the bold code:

```
$('.changeTextButton').click(function() {
   $(this).siblings('.moreText').slideToggle(500);
});
```

We want to find our div with the **moreText** class, so **.moreText** will find just that!

13. Save the file.

14. Switch to the browser and reload **history-news-jquery.html**.

15. Click a **More** button. Wowee! Isn't it amazing what a few lines of code with jQuery can do? If you wanted to write this animation from scratch without jQuery, we can assure you it wouldn't be anywhere near this easy.

---

## Swapping the Button Image with jQuery

In all your excitement, you may not have noticed that the button still says **More**, even when it's going to hide the text. We already know that **this** refers to the image, so all we need to do is check to see which image it is (either **More** or **Less**) and swap it accordingly.

1. Switch back to your code editor.

2. Below the slideToggle() animation line, add the following **if** statement:

```
   $(this).siblings('.moreText').slideToggle(500);
   if ( $(this).attr('src') == 'img/more-button.png' ) {

   }
});
```

**.attr()** looks for attributes of that element. We're looking for the image's **source** (src) and checking if it is equal to **more-button.png**. Further, if it is equal to **More**, we want to swap it with the **Less** image.

3. Add this code to set the **src** to **less-button.png**:

```
if ( $(this).attr('src') == 'img/more-button.png' ) {
   $(this).attr('src', 'img/less-button.png');
}
```

4. Save the file.

5. Switch to the browser and reload **history-news-jquery.html**.

6. Test one of the buttons. The image should change to say **Less**, but when you click it again, it won't change back to **More**.

7. Switch back to your code editor.

8. Below the **if** statement, add an **else** condition as shown in bold:

```
if ( $(this).attr('src') == 'img/more-button.png' ) {
   $(this).attr('src', 'img/less-button.png');
}
else {

}
});
```

NOTE: When the original condition of an **if** statement is false, nothing happens. You can use **else** to define what happens when the condition is false.

9. Add the following code to set the **src** to **more-button.png** (you can copy and paste the code from the less button, then change **less** to **more**):

```
if ( $(this).attr('src') == 'img/more-button.png' ) {
   $(this).attr('src', 'img/less-button.png');
}
else {
   $(this).attr('src', 'img/more-button.png');
}
```

10. That's it! Save the file.

11. Switch to the browser one last time and reload **history-news-jquery.html**.

12. Test out all the buttons.

NOTE: If you want to refer to our final code example, go to **Desktop > Class Files > yourname-JavaScript jQuery Class > Done-Files > Show-Hide-Advanced**.

_____

# Using jQuery Plugins: Smooth Scroll

## Exercise Preview

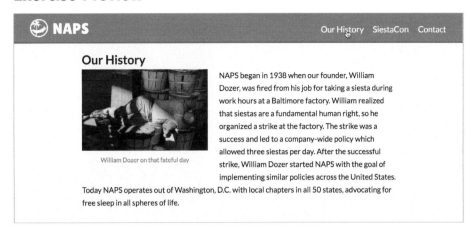

## Exercise Overview

jQuery lets developers write a bunch of jQuery code and package it together in a way that's easy for others to use the functionality. These are called plugins, and they are extremely useful and a huge time saver! They enable you to create complex interactivity with very little work on your part. Many jQuery plugins are free. Some cost money, but are cheap compared to the time it would take you to code the same functionality.

In this exercise, you'll learn how to use a jQuery plugin called Smooth Scroll. It lets you create a single page site with navigation that scrolls down the page with a sliding animation.

## Getting Started

1. Open your code editor if it isn't already open.

2. Close any files you may have open.

3. For this exercise we'll be working with the **Smooth-Scroll** folder located in **Desktop > Class Files > yourname-JavaScript jQuery Class**. You may want to open that folder in your code editor if it allows you to (like Sublime Text does).

4. Open **index.html** from the **Smooth-Scroll** folder.

5. Starting on line 17, notice that each of the three links have an href that's formatted as **#id** (#history, #siestacon, #contact).

   Each ID corresponds to a section lower in this page. We gave each section an ID and created a link to each of the three sections.

6. Preview **index.html** in a browser. This is the same page we added the random testimonial to in an earlier exercise.

JAVASCRIPT & JQUERY • COPYRIGHT NOBLE DESKTOP

7. Click the **SiestaCon** link near the top right of the page.

   You will be scrolled down to the **SiestaCon** section. While this works, it's too abrupt. We'd like the page to slide down with an animation, so users will realize they are being scrolled down the page.

8. Leave the page open in the browser so we can come back to it later.

9. Return to **index.html** in your code editor.

## Linking to the Plugin File

We've included the **Smooth Scroll** file in the class files, but you can also visit **tinyurl.com/js-smooth-scroll** to download it, read the documentation, and see examples.

As their name implies, jQuery plugins require jQuery to work. Any time we use a jQuery plugin we'll have to link to jQuery first, **before** linking to the plugin.

1. To save you some time, we've already linked to jQuery and a **main.js** where we have the JavaScript code for the random testimonial (and where we'll write our jQuery code).

   We need to link to the Smooth Scroll .js file though. On line 67, **after** the jQuery link, add the following code:

   ```
   <script src="js/jquery-2.1.0.min.js"></script>
   <script src="js/jquery.smooth-scroll.min.js"></script>
   <script src="js/main.js"></script>
   ```

2. Save the file.

## Initializing the Plugin

We've linked to all the files, so we're ready to initialize the plugin.

1. From the **js** folder, open **main.js**.

2. On line 13 notice we already have jQuery's document ready code.

3. Inside **$(document).ready**, add the following bold code to apply **smoothScroll()** to all links (**a** tags):

   ```
   $(document).ready(function() {
      $('a').smoothScroll();
   });
   ```

4. Save **main.js**.

5. Switch to your browser and reload **index.html**.

6. Click on any of the navigation buttons at the top of the page. The page should now smoothly scroll to the appropriate section of the page. Sweet!

---

## Customizing the Plugin with Options

Most jQuery plugins are customizable. The default settings for this plugin work well, but it offers some options to modify how the plugin works. You can see the features and options available on the Smooth Scroll website **tinyurl.com/js-smooth-scroll**. We want to change the speed of the scroll.

1. Switch back to **main.js** in your code editor.

2. Inside the smoothScroll parenthesis, add **{}** as shown below in bold:

   ```
   $('a').smoothScroll({});
   ```

   NOTE: Options for jQuery plugins are listed in Object syntax. The curly braces **{}** will contain the list of options. If there are multiple options, they'll be separated by commas.

3. Put the cursor inside the curly braces **{}** and hit **Return** (Mac) or **Enter** (Windows) to add an empty line, as shown below:

   ```
   $('a').smoothScroll({

   });
   ```

4. Add the following bold code:

   ```
   $('a').smoothScroll({
       speed: 1000
   });
   ```

5. Save **main.js**.

6. Switch to your browser and reload **index.html**.

7. Click on some of the navigation buttons to see that it's scrolling very slowly. Time is generally measured in milliseconds in JavaScript. The value **1000** is telling the browser to take one second (1000 milliseconds) to scroll to a given section of the page.

8. Switch back to **main.js** in your code editor.

9. Change the speed to **220** as shown in bold below:

   ```
   $('a').smoothScroll({
       speed: 220
   });
   ```

10. Save **main.js**.

11. Switch to your browser and reload **index.html**.

12. Click on some of the navigation buttons to see that the scrolling is faster. That looks great, and we only had to write few lines of code (thanks to the plugin)!

    NOTE: If you want to refer to our final code example, go to **Desktop > Class Files > yourname-JavaScript jQuery Class > Done-Files > Smooth-Scroll**.

---

**Things Common to All jQuery Plugins**

There are tons of jQuery plugins. We'll look at a few more plugins in the next exercises. They'll get a little more complicated and interesting, but plugins all have a few things in common:

1. Always link to the jQuery .js file **before** linking to the plugin's .js file.

2. The jQuery code you write to call the plugin must come **after** the link to the plugin's .js file.

3. If the plugin comes with CSS, link to the plugin's .css file **before** your own .css file (so you can override their CSS if needed).

---

## Exercise Preview

## Exercise Overview

When a user clicks a thumbnail image to see a larger version, there are numerous ways to handle what happens next. The thumbnail could link to another page, but then a user must click the Back button to return to the page. While pop-up windows can work, their appeal has been tarnished by pop-up ads and they don't work well on tablets or mobile devices.

Another option is to use JavaScript to create a "lightbox" effect. The images open within the page (over the page's content), and are user-friendly. Users can easily switch between photos with buttons or keystrokes, and close it with a button or keystroke! In this exercise, you'll learn how to use a free jQuery lightbox plugin called **Magnific Popup**.

## Getting Started

1. Open your code editor if it isn't already open.

2. Close any files you may have open.

3. For this exercise we'll be working with the **Lightbox-Gallery** folder located in **Desktop > Class Files > yourname-JavaScript jQuery Class**. You may want to open that folder in your code editor if it allows you to (like Sublime Text does).

4. Open **photo-gallery.html** from the **Lightbox-Gallery** folder.

5. Preview **photo-gallery.html** in Chrome (we'll be using its DevTools later).

6. Click some of the photos in the gallery to see that they currently are just normal links that take you to enlarged pictures. Let's spruce things up.

7. Leave the page open in Chrome so we can come back to it later.

# 5B     jQuery Lightbox: A Pop-up Image Viewer

## Linking to the Plugin Files

We've included the **Magnific Popup** file in our class files, but you can also visit **dimsemenov.com/plugins/magnific-popup** to download it, read the documentation, and see examples.

At a minimum, Magnific Popup requires three files to run—**jQuery**, the **Magnific Popup JS file**, and the **Magnific Popup CSS file**. This page already has jQuery linked, so we just need to add the Magnific Popup files. Let's link to the CSS file first.

1. Return to **photo-gallery.html** in your code editor.

2. It's important to link to the Magnific Popup CSS **before** our custom CSS. This way our CSS code will override any styling in the plugin. Above the link to **main.css** around line 6, link to the Magnific Popup CSS file as shown in bold:

   ```
   <title>The Jive Factory</title>
   <link rel="stylesheet" href="js/vendor/magnific/magnific-popup.css">
   <link rel="stylesheet" href="css/main.css">
   </head>
   ```

3. Next we'll link to the Magnific Popup JS file. Around line 109, **after** the jQuery link, add the following code:

   ```
   <script src="js/vendor/jquery-2.1.0.min.js"></script>
   <script src="js/vendor/magnific/jquery.magnific-popup.min.js"></script>
   <script src="js/main.js"></script>
   ```

4. Save the file.

## Initializing the Pop-up

1. We've linked to all the files, so we're ready to initialize Magnific Popup. We'll start with a prepared code snippet we got from the documentation on the Magnific Popup website. From the **snippets** folder, open **magnific-example.js**.

2. This code initializes the **magnificPopup()** function. When you click any link (the **a** tag), it will load an image into the pop-up. Select and copy all the code.

3. From the **js** folder, open **main.js**.

4. Put your cursor on the empty line 34 below the **// Lightbox** comment and paste the code as shown in bold:

   ```
   // Lightbox
   $('a').magnificPopup({
      type: 'image'
   });


   });
   ```

5. Save **main.js**.

6. Switch to Chrome and reload **photo-gallery.html**.

7. Click on any of the 12 thumbnails in the photo gallery to test out the lightbox. A larger photo should appear and the rest of the page will darken. Close the pop-up by clicking the **X** at the top right of the image, or by clicking outside the photo.

8. Click on **The Jive Factory** logo on the top left of the page. This should display an error that the image can't be loaded. That's because that image links to index.html and not an image. We shouldn't be targeting all links, just the links in the gallery.

9. Switch back to **main.js** in your code editor.

10. All the thumbnail images reside in a div which has the ID of **gallery**. Around line 34, change the code to target only the links inside the **gallery** div:

```
$('#gallery a').magnificPopup({
    type: 'image'
});
```

11. Save **main.js**.

12. Switch to Chrome and reload **photo-gallery.html**.

13. Click the image thumbnails and logo again. Notice that only the links to photos in the gallery get the pop-up effect. Sweet!

---

## Grouping the Photos into a Gallery

It would be nice if the photos were grouped together so that the user could go between them with next and previous buttons (or keystrokes). Magnific Popup makes this very easy!

1. Switch back to **main.js** in your code editor.

2. Add the following bold code:

```
$('#gallery a').magnificPopup({
    gallery: {
        enabled: true
    },
    type: 'image'
});
```

3. Save **main.js**.

4. Switch to Chrome and reload **photo-gallery.html**.

5. Click on any photo thumbnail to see the pop-up.

6. There should now be arrows on the left and right sides of the page. Click them to change images.

7. Press the **Left** or **Right Arrow** key on the keyboard. Nice! Users can navigate through the images with the Arrow keys or by clicking the buttons.

8. There's one more way to change photos. Click on the enlarged photo to advance to the next image.

9. Close the enlarged image using any of the following methods:

   • Click the **X** at the photo's top right corner.

   • Press the **Escape (Esc)** key.

   • Click anywhere on the page outside the enlarged image.

## Adding Captions

Magnific Popup can add captions to the enlarged images. To do this it looks at the **title** attribute of the link that is clicked. If the link has a **title**, it will add it as a caption. If there is no title, then there's no caption. None of our links currently have titles, so let's add some.

1. Switch back to your code editor.

2. Switch to **photo-gallery.html** so we can add some markup.

3. Find the code for the **#gallery** div around line 68.

4. On the first link, add the bold title attribute as shown below:

```
<div id="gallery">
   <a href="img/gallery/bugs1.jpg" title="Working Double-Time"><img src="img/
gallery/thumbs/t-bugs1.jpg"></a>
```

5. Save the file.

6. Switch to Chrome and reload **photo-gallery.html**.

7. Click on the **top left** thumbnail image. Below the enlarged image, you should see the title **Working Double-Time**.

8. Let's do another one. Back in your code editor, for the second link, add the bold code as shown below:

```
<div id="gallery">
   <a href="img/gallery/bugs1.jpg" title="Working Double-Time"><img src="img/
gallery/thumbs/t-bugs1.jpg"></a>
   <a href="img/gallery/bugs2.jpg" title="Melodica Solo"><img src="img/gallery/
thumbs/t-bugs2.jpg"></a>
```

9. Save the file.

10. Switch to Chrome, reload **photo-gallery.html**, and:

   • Again click the **top left** thumbnail image and notice the caption below the enlarged image.

   • Press the **Right Arrow** key and notice the caption changes for the next photo.

   • Press the **Right Arrow** key again and notice the caption disappears, because this photo doesn't have a title.

   • While we're looking below the image, notice on the bottom right there is an image counter. It's fine if you want it, but let's see how to remove it if you don't.

   NOTE: We could add titles (captions) to the rest of the images, but we think you get the idea, so we'll just move on.

## Removing the Counter

1. Switch back to your code editor.

2. Switch to **main.js**.

3. To remove the counter, we need to customize its text option. By setting the text to nothing, we'll remove it! Add the following bold code, but don't miss the comma at the end of the **enabled** line above it!

```
$('#gallery a').magnificPopup({
   gallery: {
      enabled: true,
      tCounter: '' // those are two single quotes!
   },
   type: 'image'
});
```

   NOTE: Options end with a comma if they are followed by another option. The last option has no end comma. Forgetting this can break the whole thing!

4. Save **main.js**.

5. Switch to Chrome and reload **photo-gallery.html**.

6. Click on the **top left** thumbnail image. The counter should not be there anymore. Keep the lightbox open, we're not done with it yet.

## Customizing the Look of the Captions

We can change the styling of the captions with CSS. First we need to find out how Magnific Popup is styling them.

## jQuery Lightbox: A Pop-up Image Viewer

1. The caption should be visible on the bottom left of the enlarged image. **Ctrl–click** (Mac) or **Right–click** (Windows) on the caption text and choose **Inspect**.

2. In the DevTools you should be able to see that the caption is wrapped by `<div class="mfp-title">` which we can target for styling!

3. While we're in the DevTools, make sure the **.mfp-title** div is selected, and on the right side notice the CSS. You should see it has **padding-right: 36px;** (to make room for the counter). We want to center the text, so now that we've removed the counter, we must also remove this padding or the text won't be properly centered.

4. Switch back to your code editor.

5. From the **css** folder, open **main.css**.

6. Below the **#contentPanel #gallery a** style around line 99, add the following:

```
.mfp-title {
    padding-right: 0;
    text-align: center;
    color: #f6cf70;
    font-weight: bold;
    text-transform: uppercase;
    font-size: 14px;
}
```

7. Save **main.css**.

8. Switch back to Chrome and reload **photo-gallery.html**.

9. Click the **top left** thumbnail image to see that the caption should now be centered, a new color, uppercase, and slightly larger than before. Keep the lightbox window open, we're not done with it yet.

---

### Customizing the Overlay's Background Color

Magnific Popup adds an overlay behind the enlarged photo to help separate it from the page's content. We can change the color of that, and we'd like to lighten it.

1. With the lightbox still open, **Ctrl–click** (Mac) or **Right–click** (Windows) outside the enlarged image (on the background) and choose **Inspect**.

2. In the DevTools, find the first tag inside the **body** tag. It should be `<div class="mfp-bg mfp-ready"></div>`.

3. Select that tag and on the right, find the **.mfp-bg** rule.

4. Notice it has a **background** of **#0b0b0b**.

5. Switch back to **main.css** in your code editor.

6. Below the **.mfp-title** style (which starts around line 105) add the following:

```
.mfp-bg {
   background: #333;
}
```

7. Save **main.css**.

8. Switch back to Chrome and reload **photo-gallery.html**.

9. Click on any thumbnail image and notice the background is now a bit lighter. Keep the lightbox window open, we're not done with it yet.

## Customizing the Look of the Arrows

1. While you still have the lightbox open, notice the arrows have a faint outline around them. It's very close in color to the background, so you may not be able to see it depending on the brightness and contrast of your monitor. Don't worry if you can't see it, but know that we can change the fill or outline color of the arrows. Let's do that next!

2. **Ctrl–click** (Mac) or **Right–click** (Windows) on the lightbox's **right arrow (next)** and choose **Inspect**.

3. In the DevTools, expand the **button** element to see the **::before** and **::after** elements inside.

```
       ...</button>
...   ▼<button title="Next (Right arrow key)" type="button"
        class="mfp-arrow mfp-arrow-right mfp-prevent-close"> == $0
          ::before
          ::after
       </button>
```

NOTE: The **::before** element is the outline and the **::after** element is the fill.

4. Select the **::before** element.

5. In the **Styles** on the right, find the .mfp-arrow-right:before rule and notice that it has a property declaration of: **border-left: 27px solid #3f3f3f;**

6. Select the **::after** element.

7. In the **Styles** on the right, find the .mfp-arrow-right:after rule and notice that it has the following property declaration: **border-left: 17px solid white;**.

   To adjust the color of the fill and outline we can change these two elements. If we made you manually style these, you'd do a bunch of copying and pasting class names, colors, etc. so we've saved you some time and made a snippet.

8. Switch back to your code editor.

9. From the **snippets** folder, open **magnific-arrow-colors.css**.

10. Select and copy all the code.

11. Switch back to **main.css**.

12. Paste the new rules below the **.mfp-bg** rule (which starts around line 113).

    NOTE: You can use this snippet in your own projects, but you'll want to customize the colors to fit your design.

13. Save **main.css**.

14. Switch to Chrome and reload **photo-gallery.html**.

15. Click on any thumbnail image and notice the arrow colors better fit our design. Hover over them and notice the opacity changes so they appear brighter.

16. All that's left to do is customize the color of the **close X** button at the top right. **Ctrl–click** (Mac) or **Right–click** (Windows) on it and choose **Inspect**.

17. In the DevTools you should see a **button** element with a class of **mfp-close**. That's what we can target with CSS.

## Customizing the Look of the X Close Button

1. Switch back to **main.css** in your code editor.

2. Below the **.mfp-bg** style (which starts around line 113) add the following:

```
.mfp-close {
    color: #f6cf70;
}
```

3. Save the file.

4. Switch back to Chrome and reload **photo-gallery.html**.

5. Click on any thumbnail image and notice the **close X** is still white, instead of the yellow we want. Why didn't our style work?

6. **Ctrl–click** (Mac) or **Right–click** (Windows) on the **close X** button and choose **Inspect**.

7. With the **mfp-close button** selected in the code, look in the **Styles** on the right. The name of the rule with the **color: white** property declaration is **.mfp-image-holder .mfp-close**.

    By specifying the extra container's class, their rule is more specific than ours and overrides our CSS. Luckily that's easy to fix.

8. Switch back to your code editor.

9. Around line 116, add another selector to the **.mfp-close** rule as shown in bold below:

```
.mfp-image-holder .mfp-close {
   color: #f6cf70;
}
```

10. Save the file.

11. Switch to Chrome and reload **photo-gallery.html**.

12. Click on any thumbnail image and notice the close X is now yellow. Lookin' good!

NOTE: If you want to refer to our final code example, go to **Desktop > Class Files > yourname-JavaScript jQuery Class > Done-Files > Lightbox-Gallery**.

---

**fancyBox: Another Good Lightbox**

There are tons of jQuery lightboxes. All of them work pretty similarly, but we're not thrilled by all of them. Some aren't attractive, or have slow animations that are annoying as a user. One lightbox we particularly like is fancyBox. You can learn more at **fancyapps.com/fancybox** and try it out for free. It's free for personal use and non-profit websites. For commercial use you can purchase a license for one website for just $19 or for unlimited websites for $89.

While Magnific loads faster, two things that set fancyBox apart is how it animates the lightbox. It can animate open and closed. Magnific's Zoom option doesn't animate things open unless they are preloaded (which they aren't until you've opened them). Secondly, fancyBox has a thumbnail option not found in Magnific. It's a nice alternative. Both are great, so use whichever suits your needs best!

---

## Exercise Preview

## Exercise Overview

In this exercise, you'll learn how to use the jQuery Cycle plugin to create a simple slideshow. It can cycle through content with a variety of transitions like fades, pushes, etc. This allows you to display many items in a small space (but one at a time) without the user having to do anything. The next slide is automatically displayed after a time delay of your choosing.

---

## Getting Started

1. Open your code editor if it isn't already open.

2. Close any files you may have open.

3. For this exercise we'll be working with the **Cycle-Simple-Slideshow** folder located in **Desktop > Class Files > yourname-JavaScript jQuery Class**. You may want to open that folder in your code editor if it allows you to (like Sublime Text does).

4. Open **index.html** from the **Cycle-Simple-Slideshow** folder.

5. Preview **index.html** in Chrome (we'll be using its DevTools).

6. Towards the bottom of the page, **Ctrl–click** (Mac) or **Right–click** (Windows) on the **Jive T-Shirts** image, and choose **Inspect**.

7. The DevTools will open at the bottom of the window. As shown below, select the **subContent1** div on the left side of the DevTools.

```
►<div id="accordionNav">…</div>
►<div id="content">…</div>
▼<div id="subContent1" class="subColumn">
    <img src="img/ad-tshirt.jpg">
    <img src="img/ad-happy.jpg">
    <img src="img/ad-reserve.jpg">
  </div>
►<div id="subContent2" class="subColumn">…</div>
►<div id="subContent3" class="subColumn">…</div>
```

8. We want each of the three subContent sections at the bottom of the page to cycle through related content. Each column is a div that contains hidden content. We'll use the **Cycle** plugin to display the hidden content, but first let's see that hidden content. On the right side of the DevTools, find the **.subColumn** style.

9. As shown below, mouse over **height** and uncheck the property.

10. Close the DevTools.

11. Scroll down the page and notice that you can see a bunch of previously hidden content such as **Happy Hour**, **Private Jive**, **Our Philosophy**, etc.

    NOTE: If you have multiple elements in a slideshow, it's possible the extra elements will be visible for a short time when the page first loads. Once the Cycle JS loads, it will hide the extra elements, but in the meantime you may see a brief flash of unstyled content (FOUC). To avoid this, you can use CSS to hide everything except the first one (which is what we've already done by setting a **height** on the container and setting **overflow: hidden**). In the next exercise, we'll look closer at another technique for doing this.

12. Switch back to your code editor.

---

## Initial Setup

We've already downloaded the Cycle plugin and included it in our class files. At **malsup.com/jquery/cycle2** you can download the files, find useful documentation, examples, and other support. It's another free plugin, but we encourage you to donate to its creator if you like it!

1. Now that we know the page is ready with the content we want to be cycled, we can make it actually happen. Switch back to **index.html** in your code editor.

2. We need to add links to some script files. The preferred order of linking is jQuery, plugins, then your JS files. Around line 93, before the link to **main.js** add the following two bold links:

```
</div>
<script src="js/vendor/jquery-2.1.0.min.js"></script>
<script src="js/vendor/cycle/jquery.cycle2.min.js"></script>
<script src="js/main.js"></script>
</body>
```

3. Save the file.

## Defining What Content Gets Cycled

1. From the **js** folder open **main.js**.

2. On line 30 notice we already have jQuery's **document ready** code. We only need one instance of this, so we can add our jQuery code inside it.

3. From the **snippets** folder open **cycle-example.js**.

4. Select all the code.

5. Copy it and close the file.

6. On line 33, below the **// Cycles** comment within the **document ready** braces, paste the code so it appears as below:

```
// Cycles
$('element').cycle({
    fx: 'effectName',
    speed: 300,
    timeout: 1000,
    delay: 0
});

});
```

7. Let's customize this to cycle through our first subContent div, which we gave an ID of **subContent1**. Make the following changes in bold:

```
// Cycles
$('#subContent1').cycle({
    fx: 'scrollHorz',
    speed: 300,
    timeout: 1000,
    delay: 0
});
```

8. Save the file.

9. Preview **index.html** in a browser. Watch for the sliding animated content!

10. Leave the page open in the browser so we can come back to it later.

11. Let's slow down the cycling. Switch back to **main.js** in your code editor.

12. Change the **timeout** amount to **4000**.

    NOTE: Timeout is the amount of time between each cycle. It's measured in milliseconds, so each **1000** is equal to 1 second. **4000** is 4 seconds.

13. Save the file.

14. Switch to the browser and reload **index.html**.

15. That's much better, but the animation itself is quick and a bit jarring. Let's slow that down. Switch back to **main.js** in your code editor.

16. Change the **speed** to **600**.

    NOTE: Speed is the amount of time the transition takes. It's also measured in milliseconds, so a speed of **600** is 0.6 seconds.

17. Save the file.

18. Switch to the browser and reload **index.html**. Excellent.

---

## Adding More Cycles & Exploring Options

1. Switch back to **main.js** in your code editor.

2. Select the entire **cycle()** code shown below:

```
$('#subContent1').cycle({
    fx: 'scrollHorz',
    speed: 600,
    timeout: 4000,
    delay: 0
});
```

3. Copy it.

4. Paste a copy directly below it. Make sure it's still above the end **});** braces and within the document ready function.

5. This time, we'll do a **fade** transition. Fade is the default effect if none is specified, so we can remove the **fx** setting. **Delete** the **fx** line so you have the following code:

```
$('#subContent1').cycle({
    speed: 600,
    timeout: 4000,
    delay: 0
});
```

6. Now we have to target the proper element. In the pasted code, change **subContent1** to **subContent2**:

```
$('#subContent2').cycle({
   speed: 600,
   timeout: 4000,
   delay: 0
});
```

7. Save the file.

8. Switch to the browser and reload **index.html**.

9. Wait a moment and watch for **What's The Jive?** to change. You'll see that **Jive T-Shirts** animates, but **What's The Jive?** doesn't. Why?

   The Cycle plugin looks for images inside the parent div. In **subContent1** (on the left) we have nested **img** tags. But in **subContent2** (in the middle) we have nested **div** tags. Cycle can work with nested div tags, but we must tell it to look for them instead of img tags.

10. Switch back to **main.js** in your code editor.

11. Add the following line of code shown in bold:

```
$('#subContent2').cycle({
   slides: '> div',
   speed: 600,
   timeout: 4000,
   delay: 0
});
```

   NOTE: We give the **slides** option a jQuery selector. **Parent > child** in CSS means to find the immediate children of the parent, without finding further nested elements. So **'> div'** finds div tags that are children of the element we're currently giving to the cycle (which in this case is **#subContent2**) without finding div tags inside of those div tags.

12. Save the file.

13. Switch to the browser and reload **index.html**.

14. Wait a moment to see it fade from **What's The Jive?** to **Our Philosophy**.

15. Switch back to your code editor.

16. Select the entire **subContent1** cycle code. That's the first one, not the second!

17. Copy it.

18. Paste a copy below the **subContent2** version. Make sure it's still above the end **});** braces and within the document ready function.

19. Let's do a different scroll effect for this one. In the code you just pasted (the third and last cycle), change both the name of the element and effect name as shown below in bold:

```
$('#subContent3').cycle({
    fx: 'scrollVert',
    speed: 600,
    timeout: 4000,
    delay: 0
});
```

20. Save the file.

21. This transition is not included in the core Cycle JS file. It's available as a separate file which we've already downloaded for you and added into this site. Switch to **index.html** so we can link to it.

22. At the bottom, around line 94, find the Cycle plugin's **script** tag. Add the following bold code underneath it as shown:

```
<script src="js/vendor/jquery-2.1.0.min.js"></script>
<script src="js/vendor/cycle/jquery.cycle2.min.js"></script>
<script src="js/vendor/cycle/transitions/jquery.cycle2.scrollVert.min.js">
</script>
<script src="js/main.js"></script>
</body>
```

23. Save the file.

24. Switch to the browser and reload **index.html**. Wait a moment to see **Premium Jive** change to **Battle of the Bands**.

    It's a little silly having all the cycles change at the same time. The **delay** option can take care of that by pausing before the first animation, making it start later. Setting a different delay for each one will stagger the animations. Return to your code editor.

25. Switch to **main.js** in your code editor.

26. In the **subContent1** cycle code, set the **delay** to **1000**.

27. Save the file.

28. Switch to the browser and reload **index.html**.

    Notice that the animations don't all happen at the same time now.

29. Switch back to your code editor.

30. In the **subContent2** cycle code, set the **delay** to **4000**.

31. In the **subContent3** cycle code, set the **delay** to **2500**.

32. Save the file, switch to the browser, and reload **index.html**. Awesome!

## Reversing the Animation

Currently, the horizontal animation moves from right to left and the vertical moves from top to bottom. But what if we wanted them to go in the opposite direction? That's easy, so let's see how.

1. Switch back to your code editor.

2. On the third cycle, add the following line of bold code:

```
$('#subContent3').cycle({
    fx: 'scrollVert',
    reverse: 'true',
    speed: 600,
    timeout: 4000,
    delay: 2500
});
```

   NOTE: This same option will work on **scrollHorz** as well.

3. Save the file and switch to the browser to reload **index.html**. Notice that the right column should now animate from bottom to top now.

## Optional Bonus Challenge: Exploring Other Transitions

In addition to **scrollVert**, there are some other optional transitions that you can load and use. As a challenge, see if you can use a different transition without specific instructions. Here's the general idea:

1. Link **index.html** to the appropriate **.js** transition script. You will find the files in **Cycle-Simple-Slideshow > js > vendor > cycle > transitions**.

2. In **main.js** change the **fx** option to one of the following:

   - flipVert

   - flipHorz

   - tileSlide

   - tileBlind

   If you need any help, refer to the demos at **jquery.malsup.com/cycle2/demo**

   NOTE: If you want to refer to our final code example, go to **Desktop > Class Files > yourname-JavaScript jQuery Class > Done-Files > Cycle-Simple-Slideshow**.

## Two Ways to Code Cycles

The Cycle jQuery plugin is a bit unique in that it can be coded two different ways. This exercise focused on using JavaScript to set what elements will be cycled and the options for how the cycles work. The other way you can define cycles is a declarative method which focuses purely on HTML. This is how most of the Cycle website's documentation is written. This approach has you do the following:

1. Link to the Cycle JS file(s). You don't need to write any JavaScript yourself. No script tag or document.ready is needed.

2. Add a **class="cycle-slideshow"** to the container. The Cycle plugin will automatically find these containers and start the cycles on them.

3. Add **data-cycle-*** attributes to the container to set options.

Which coding method you choose is partially based on personal preference. Writing the JavaScript (as we did in this exercise) keeps your HTML clean and allows you to easily reuse the options across elements within a page or across many webpages. It also gives you more control. Using the declarative style (with HTML classes and attributes) is easier for those not comfortable with JavaScript, which is maybe why Cycle's website prefers it (so they don't get as many support emails). It's OK for simple stuff, but doesn't offer some of the control that we'll need in later exercises.

**Exercise Preview**

**Exercise Overview**

In the previous exercise, you learned how to create a simple slideshow using the jQuery Cycle plugin. In this exercise, you'll add controls to a slideshow which will allow the end user to jump ahead or back to specific slides.

## Getting Started

1. Open your code editor if it isn't already open.

2. Close any files you may have open.

3. For this exercise we'll be working with the **Cycle-Slideshow-Controls** folder located in **Desktop > Class Files > yourname-JavaScript jQuery Class**. You may want to open that folder in your code editor if it allows you to (like Sublime Text does).

4. Open **index.html** from the **Cycle-Slideshow-Controls** folder.

5. Preview the page in a browser to see what the page will look like to users.

   We want to turn the main photo into a slideshow highlighting upcoming events. The other images for this section are not yet in the page, so first we must insert them.

6. Leave the page open in the browser so we can come back to it later.

7. Switch back to your code editor.

8. Find the **featuredShows** div around line 66 and notice that this div currently only has one image.

9. Add the following bold code to add the rest of the slideshow images:

```
<div id="featuredShows">
    <img src="img/scroll-lustre.jpg" width="530" height="375">
    <img src="img/scroll-bugs.jpg" width="530" height="375">
    <img src="img/scroll-blast.jpg" width="530" height="375">
    <img src="img/scroll-battle.jpg" width="530" height="375">
</div>
```

10. Save the file.

11. Switch to the browser and reload **index.html**. Notice that you can see all four band photos (Low Lustre, Lightning Bug, etc.) stacked on top of each other.

## Preventing a Possible "Flash of Unstyled Content"

Once we get the Cycle plugin working, it will hide the additional slideshow photos and start cycling through them. The cycle doesn't start until the JS files have been downloaded. That may take a moment, and in the meantime, a user may see all four photos. When the Cycle plugin kicks in, the page will abruptly hide the extra photos and start the cycle.

We can avoid this flash of unstyled content (FOUC) with CSS. We simply hide the extra photos initially, so users won't see them. The Cycle plugin will unhide them when it has loaded and is ready to put them into the slideshow.

1. Switch back to your code editor.

2. From the **css** folder, open **main.css** (remember we're in the **Cycle-Slideshow-Controls** folder).

3. Below the **#featuredShows** rule that starts around line 87, add the following:

```
#featuredShows img {
    display: none;
}
#featuredShows img:first-child {
    display: block;
}
```

4. Save the file.

5. Switch to the browser and reload **index.html**. You should now only see one photo (Low Lustre). We'll see the other photos after we get the Cycle plugin working.

## Enabling the Slideshow

1. Switch back to your code editor.

2. Our page is already linked to jQuery and the Cycle plugin .js files because we added them in the previous exercise. That means we're ready to add the JavaScript to apply the cycle to the **#featuredShows** div. From the **js** folder, open **main.js**.

3. Around lines 33–38 select the **subContent1** cycle code.

4. Copy it.

5. Paste a copy below the last cycle, making sure it's still above the last set of **});** braces and within the document ready function.

6. The images we just added are in a div which has an ID of **featuredShows**. Make the following three edits to the copy just added: target the **featuredShows** div, set it to advance slides every 3 seconds (a **3000** millisecond **timeout**) with no initial **delay** (so the slide counter starts right away):

```
$('#featuredShows').cycle({
    fx: 'scrollHorz',
    speed: 600,
    timeout: 3000,
    delay: 0
});
```

7. Lastly, we want the slideshow to use a fade transition, so **delete** the **fx** line of code so you end up with the following:

```
$('#featuredShows').cycle({
    speed: 600,
    timeout: 3000,
    delay: 0
});
```

8. Save the file.

9. Switch to the browser and reload **index.html**. Wait a few seconds to see the other photos fade in one after another!

## Adding & Customizing the Controls

A user might want to go back to see a specific slide again. The plugin has built-in features to make controls. To use it we need a div with a **cycle-pager** class (which the plugin automatically looks for).

1. Switch to **index.html** in your code editor.

2. We don't have a place to hold the controls yet, so we'll have to make one. Before the **#featuredShows** closing div tag around line 71, add the following bold code:

```
<div id="content">
   <div id="featuredShows">
      <img src="img/scroll-lustre.jpg" width="530" height="375">
      <img src="img/scroll-bugs.jpg" width="530" height="375">
      <img src="img/scroll-blast.jpg" width="530" height="375">
      <img src="img/scroll-battle.jpg" width="530" height="375">
      <div class="cycle-pager"></div>
   </div>
</div>
```

NOTE: The Cycle plugin automatically looks for a div with the **cycle-pager** class within the slideshow container and creates slide indicators inside it! This works great when the slideshow content is images, like we have. If your content was div tags, you'd have to move the pager outside the slideshow container and tell Cycle about it. For more info on that, refer to the sidebar at the end of this exercise.

3. Save the file.

4. Switch to the browser and reload **index.html**.

   On the bottom left of the main slideshow you should see four very small white dots. They are too small to use, and there is no indication of which one is the current slide, so we need to add some CSS to improve the design.

5. Switch back to your code editor.

6. The dots are bullet characters, so we can change their size with the CSS **font-size** property. To save some time, we've already written out a style for you. In the **snippets** folder, open **cycle-pager-style.css**.

7. Select and copy all the code.

8. From the **css** folder, open **main.css**.

9. Around line 94, find the **#featuredShows img:first-child** rule. Paste the new rule below that.

   NOTE: **z-index: 200;** makes sure the div is at the top of the stacking order on the page, so it will be layered visually on top of all other elements. Everything else is unique to how we want our pager to look. For your own site, you would adjust as desired.

10. Save the file.

11. Preview **index.html** in Chrome. (We're going to use its DevTools.)

12. Click the bullets to jump to a specific slide.

13. While the bullets work, notice the following problems that we need to fix:

    • There is no indication of which slide you are currently viewing.

    • When you mouse over the bullets, you see a text cursor rather than a pointer hand which would indicate a clickable item.

    • If you double–click a bullet, it selects the bullet (like a text selection), which is not desirable.

    • The bullets are a bit close together.

14. Let's see what the Cycle plugin is doing in the **cycle-pager** div. **Ctrl–click** (Mac) or **Right–click** (Windows) on one of the white bullets and from the menu that appears, choose **Inspect**.

15. As shown below, notice there are **span** tags inside the **cycle-pager**. Also, as you watch the code, the **cycle-pager-active** class will move from **span** to **span**. The Cycle plugin is adding this class, which we will be able use to style the bullet of the current (or active) slide.

```
▼<div class="cycle-pager">
    <span class>•</span>
    <span class>•</span>
    <span class="cycle-pager-active">•</span>
    <span class>•</span>
</div>
```

16. Switch back to **main.css** in your code editor.

17. Below the **.cycle-pager** rule (which starts around line 97), add the following:

```
.cycle-pager span {
    margin-right: 5px;
    cursor: pointer;
    -webkit-user-select: none;
    -moz-user-select: none;
    -ms-user-select: none;
}
```

18. Save the file.

19. Switch to the browser, reload **index.html**, and notice that:

    • The bullets should be a bit farther apart.

    • There is now a hand cursor when you mouse over them.

    • Double–clicking a bullet will not select anything.

20. All that's left to do is indicate which bullet is active! Switch back to **main.css** in your code editor.

21. Below the **.cycle-pager span** rule (which starts around line 112), add the following bold rule:

```
.cycle-pager span.cycle-pager-active {
   color: #fbc324;
}
```

22. Save the file.

23. Switch to the browser and reload **index.html**. The active slide bullet should now appear yellow. Sweet!

24. Click on the bullet controls and enjoy the completed slideshow.

   NOTE: If you want to refer to our final code example, go to **Desktop > Class Files > yourname-JavaScript jQuery Class > Done-Files > Cycle-Slideshow-Controls**.

---

**Defining a Custom Pager Outside the Slideshow Container**

The Cycle plugin automatically looks for a div with the cycle-pager class within the slideshow container. This works with images, but if your slideshow content is div tags, putting the cycle-pager div inside the slideshow container would mean the pager becomes one of the slides. Oops! In that case, you should put the pager div outside the slideshow container and give it a unique class or ID. In your JS code, you would add the following pager option to tell Cycle to use your custom pager:

```
$('#featuredShows').cycle({
   slides: '> div',
   pager: '.your-custom-cycle-pager-name',
   speed: 600,
   timeout: 3000,
   delay: 0
});
```

---

# jQuery Form Validation

## Exercise Preview

## Exercise Overview

Form validation is essential for so many websites. Here we'll show you how to set up form validation with the popular **jQuery Validation Plugin** by **Jörn Zaefferer**, which is easy, fast, flexible, and well-documented.

---

## Getting Started

1. Open your code editor if it isn't already open.

2. Close any files you may have open.

3. For this exercise we'll be working with the **Form-Validation** folder located in **Desktop > Class Files > yourname-JavaScript jQuery Class**. You may want to open that folder in your code editor if it allows you to (like Sublime Text does).

4. Open **application.html** from the **Form-Validation** folder.

5. Preview the file in a browser.

6. Without filling out the form, click **Create My Account**. You'll be taken to a Thank You page. Obviously, this form needs some validation so that users fill out the proper information.

7. Hit the back button to return to the form and leave the page open in the browser so you can reload the page as you make changes to the code.

## Initializing the Plugin & Setting Options

The **jQuery Validation Plugin** by **Jörn Zaefferer** is one of the most popular validation plugins, used by major sites all over the world. We have included it with our class files, but to download future updates, view examples, and read the documentation, go to **jqueryvalidation.org**

1. Return to your code editor.

2. We need to link to the validation plugin. In between the link to jQuery and the link to main.js (around line 67), add the following bold code:

```
<script src="js/vendor/jquery-2.1.0.min.js"></script>
<script src="js/vendor/jquery.validate.min.js"></script>
<script src="js/main.js"></script>
```

3. Save the file.

Now that we've linked to the appropriate plugin, we're ready to initialize it. A single line of jQuery is all we'll need to select the form and apply the validation plugin.

4. Open **main.js** from the **js** folder in **Form-Validation**.

5. Our form has the ID **startAccount**. Toward the bottom of the file, add this code:

```
    // Form Validation
    $('#startAccount').validate();

});
```

This says to validate the **startAccount** form. Pretty easy so far, right?

6. As shown in bold below, add a set of curly braces **{}** inside the **validate()** method's parentheses. These will group all the options we'll add next.

```
$('#startAccount').validate({});
```

7. In between the curly braces of the **validate()** method, add the bold code below:

```
$('#startAccount').validate({
    rules: {

    }
});
```

8. We've already assigned the name values of the inputs in the HTML markup. Now all we have to do is tell the jQuery plugin which elements of the form should be required by targeting the values of the **name** attributes for each input. We'll start with the **name** field. Add the bold code shown below:

```
$('#startAccount').validate({
    rules: {
        name: 'required'
    }
});
```

9. Save the file.

10. Switch to the browser and reload **application.html**.

11. Without filling out the form, click **Create My Account**. Look closely to see a message that says, **This field is required**. The validation plugin puts the error message **after** the input that has the error. This looks quite confusing, as it sits on the same line as the label for Email Address. We'll remedy this shortly.

12. For now, start typing your name into the field and you'll see the message disappear. Cool beans!

13. Let's add the other required fields. Switch back to your code editor.

14. Add the following bold code. Don't forget the **commas** after the first two options!

```
$('#startAccount').validate({
    rules: {
        name: 'required',
        email: 'required',
        phone: 'required'
    }
});
```

15. Save the file.

16. Switch to the browser and reload **application.html**.

17. Without filling out the form, click **Create My Account**. Now all the fields except the Comments are required, which is fine because comments are optional.

18. Type anything into the Email field. It will immediately validate, no matter what you type. We'd like to set the plugin up so that it will check to see if the user inputs a proper email address.

19. Switch back to your code editor.

20. Next to **email**, delete **'required'** and replace it with curly braces **{}**, as follows:

```
rules: {
    name: 'required',
    email: {},
    phone: 'required'
}
```

21. Now we can set more options for the **email** field. Inside the **{}**, set the email to **required** and tell the validation plugin that a valid email address is required by typing the bold code shown below:

```
rules: {
    name: 'required',
    email: {
        required: true,
        email: true
    },
    phone: 'required'
}
```

22. Save the file.

23. Switch to the browser and reload **application.html**.

24. Click **Create My Account**, then try typing into the Email field again. This time you'll notice that, as you begin to type, the message changes to **Please enter a valid email address**. Great!

    A valid email follows the pattern of **something@something.something**. After you type what appears to be a valid email address, the error message disappears.

---

## Customizing the Error Messages

1. Switch back to your code editor.

2. Let's add some customized error messages. Add the bold code shown below. Don't forget the **comma** and **{}** curly braces!

```
$('#startAccount').validate({
    rules: {

        ( CODE OMITTED TO SAVE SPACE )

    },
    messages: {

    }
});
```

3.  Now let's put in the messages we want. Add the bold code shown below:

```
messages: {
    name: 'Required',
    email: 'A valid email is required',
    phone: 'Required'
}
```

4.  Save the file.

5.  Switch to the browser and reload **application.html**.

6.  Without filling out the form, click **Create My Account**. You should see all your custom messages!

## Changing the Location of the Error Messages

By default, the form validation plugin puts error messages after their input fields. Instead, we'd like to move the error messages before them, next to the form labels. We can use the **errorPlacement** option to change the location.

1.  Switch back to your code editor.

2.  Below the **messages** option, add the bold code shown below. Don't forget the **comma** and **curly braces**!

```
messages: {
    name: 'Required',
    email: 'A valid email is required',
    phone: 'Required'
},
errorPlacement: function(error, element) {

}
```

The **errorPlacement** option accepts a function as its value. The parameter **error** is the error message, and **element** is the form element that caused the error. By default, the **error** message is added **after** the input element.

3.  Instead, we want to insert the error message **before** the input. Add the bold code shown below:

```
errorPlacement: function(error, element) {
    error.insertBefore();
}
```

The **insertBefore()** function says to insert the error before "something." We want that "something" to be the element that is causing the error.

4. Add the bold code shown below:

```
errorPlacement: function(error, element) {
    error.insertBefore( element );
}
```

This says to insert the error message before the element that causes the error. Our **input** fields cause the error, so this code will insert the error **before** the input. Perfect!

5. Save the file.

6. Switch to the browser and reload **application.html**.

7. Without filling out the form, click **Create My Account**. You'll see that the error messages are now **before** the inputs, as requested.

## Styling the Error Messages

The error messages are wrapped in a **label** tag by default. If you use the DevTools Inspect feature, you'll see that the plugin also assigns an **error** class to them. To style them, we need to create a style called **label.error**.

1. Switch back to your code editor.

2. Open **main.css** from the **css** folder in **Form-Validation**.

3. Scroll to the bottom of the document and add the following rule:

```
label.error {
    color: #f00;
}
```

4. Save the file.

5. Switch to the browser and reload **application.html**.

6. Without filling out the form, click **Create My Account**. Nice, hard to miss red errors!

7. Let's finish styling the errors. Switch back to **main.css** in your code editor.

8. Edit the **label.error** style by adding the following property declarations:

```
label.error {
    color: #f00;
    font-size: 10px;
    text-transform: uppercase;
    margin-left: 5px;
}
```

9. Save the file.

10. Switch to the browser and reload **application.html**. Without filling out the form, click **Create My Account**. Looking much better.

    It would also be nice to highlight the input fields. Luckily the plugin attaches an **error** class to the input fields as well, so this is very easy.

11. Switch back to your code editor.

12. After the **label.error** rule, add the following rule:

```
input.error {
    background-color: #fcffad;
}
```

13. Save the file.

14. Switch to the browser and reload **application.html**. Without filling out the form, click **Create My Account**. Now the required input fields are highlighted too, improving the usability of the page.

## Optional Bonus: Setting a Default Error Message

In our current form, we're specifying every error message. What if you have a very long form? It would be a pain to have to set every single one. There is a default message, but it might not be exactly what you want. Let's see how to set a custom default message.

1. Return to your code editor.

2. Switch to **main.js**.

3. Go to the **validate()** method and delete the **messages** for **name** and **phone** (around lines 19 and 21). We can leave the email message because we'd like it to be custom. The **messages** option should look as shown below. Don't forget to delete the **comma** after the email!

```
messages: {
    email: 'A valid email is required'
},
```

4. Save the file.

5. Switch to the browser and reload **application.html**.

6. Without filling out the form, click **Create My Account**. You'll see that the default error messages are being displayed again. We want to change them, but before we do so, let's look at the plugin's default messages in the JavaScript Console.

7. Switch back to **main.js** in your code editor.

8. The default messages are stored in **$.validator.messages**. Before the **$ ('#startAccount').validate** code around line 9, add the following bold test code so we can see what's inside it:

```
// Form Validation
console.log( $.validator.messages );
$('#startAccount').validate({
    rules: {
```

9. Save the file.

10. Preview **application.html** in Chrome (we'll be using its DevTools).

11. Hit **Cmd–Opt–J** (Mac) or **Ctrl–Shift–J** (Windows) to bring up the Console.

12. Click on **Object** in the Console to explore its contents. These are the default messages. Towards the bottom of the list is the default **required** message that we want to change. Excellent.

13. Leave the file open in Chrome, with the Console still open as well. We'll reload the page as we make changes to the code.

14. Return to your code editor.

15. Change the log to access the **required** message (around line 9):

```
console.log( $.validator.messages.required );
```

16. Save the file.

17. Return to Chrome and reload the page.

   You should see the default required message displayed. We can change this default message with a single line of code!

18. Switch back to **main.js** in your code editor.

19. Remove the **console.log()** code (around line 9) and in its place, assign a new required message as follows:

```
$.validator.messages.required = 'Required';
```

20. Save the file.

21. Return to Chrome and reload the page. Without filling out the form, click **Create My Account**. You'll now see your custom "Required" error messages.

   NOTE: If you want to refer to our final code example, go to **Desktop > Class Files > yourname-JavaScript jQuery Class > Done-Files > Form-Validation**.

## Exercise Preview

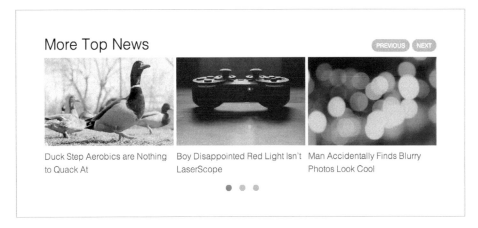

## Exercise Overview

Carousels are one way to present a series of images and/or text for users to scroll through. The free OWL Carousel plugin makes creating these easy.

---

## Linking to the Plugin Files

1. Open your code editor if it isn't already open.

2. Close any files you may have open.

3. For this exercise we'll be working with the **Carousel** folder located in **Desktop > Class Files > yourname-JavaScript jQuery Class**. You may want to open that folder in your code editor if it allows you to (like Sublime Text does).

4. Open **index.html** from the **Carousel** folder.

5. To save you some time, we've already linked to **jQuery** and **main.js** for you, but you need to link to the OWL Carousel script. On line 88, add the bold link shown below:

```
</div>
<script src="js/vendor/jquery-2.1.0.min.js"></script>
<script src="js/vendor/owl-carousel/owl.carousel.min.js"></script>
<script src="js/main.js"></script>
</body>
```

NOTE: We have included the OWL Carousel files with our class files, but to download future updates, view examples, and read documentation, you can visit **owlgraphic.com/owlcarousel**

6. The script file will create the carousel functionality, but we also need some CSS to style it. Scroll up to the top of the code.

7. On line 7, after the link to **normalize.css** add the following bold code:

```
<link rel="stylesheet" href="css/normalize.css">
<link rel="stylesheet" href="js/vendor/owl-carousel/owl.carousel.css">
<link rel="stylesheet" href="js/vendor/owl-carousel/owl.theme.css">
<link rel="stylesheet" href="css/main.css">
</head>
```

8. Save the file.

## Creating the Carousel

A carousel displays multiple items. Each item can have any content you like (images, text, etc.) but you want to wrap all the content for an item in a **div** tag. All of the item **div** tags should be wrapped in a parent **div** tag with a class of **owl-carousel**. Here's a simple example of what we mean:

```
<div class="owl-carousel">
   <div> Any Type of Content </div>
   <div> Any Type of Content </div>
   ...
</div>
```

1. We've already coded up lots of items to save you time. Starting around line 33, find the **#moreTopNews** div and look at all the **.item** divs inside it. Notice the following:

   • We added the **item** class so we'll later be able to style the divs, but it's not a requirement for OWL Carousel.

   • Each item contains an image and a heading.

   • The content in each item is wrapped in a link. In our example files, we have not built all the linked pages, but that won't matter for building the carousel. (Just don't bother clicking any of those links in a browser because you'd get a missing page error.)

2. Preview **index.html** in a browser and scroll down to the **More Top News** heading. Currently, all the items are large and you have to scroll down to see them all. This is the content for our carousel.

3. Leave the page open in the browser so we can come back to it later.

4. Switch back to your code editor.

5. Any div that is used for an OWL Carousel must have an **owl-carousel** class, so it will get some styling (such as hiding the carousel to avoid a flash of unstyled content). Around line 33, find the **#moreTopNews** div and add the bold class:

```
<div id="moreTopNews" class="owl-carousel">
```

6. Save the file.

7. Switch to the browser and reload **index.html**. Scroll down to the **More Top News** heading. Notice that the content is hidden! Don't worry, once we get the carousel working it will come back!

8. Switch back to your code editor.

9. From the **js** folder open **main.js**.

10. To initialize the OWL Carousel, add the following bold code:

```
$(document).ready(function() {

    // Carousel
    $('#moreTopNews').owlCarousel();

});
```

11. Save the file.

12. Switch to the browser and reload **index.html**. Aside from the images being cropped because they are too large, we have a working carousel! Do the following:

    • Click the gray bullets below the carousel to switch sections.

    • Drag directly on the carousel content (images or text) to move around. Not only does dragging work on mobile devices, it works on desktops too. Cool!

    • Slowly resize the window and pay attention to how many items are displayed in the carousel. As the window gets narrower, fewer items are displayed. As it gets wider, more items are displayed. That's because this carousel is responsive by default. That's awesome, but in this page (which isn't responsive) we'll want to control how many items are displayed.

    • Notice there are no previous or next buttons, which would be nice.

## Styling the Carousel

1. Switch back to your code editor.

2. Let's style the images so they will scale down to fit into the carousel. From the **css** folder, open **main.css**.

3. Below the **#moreTopNews h3** rule that starts around line 82, add the following:

```
#moreTopNews img {
    width: 100%;
}
```

4. Save the file.

5. Switch to the browser and reload **index.html**. Notice that the carousel looks much better with appropriately-sized images!

6. It looks nice with the photos touching each other, but our design calls for some space between them. Switch back to **main.css** in your code editor.

7. Below the **#moreTopNews img** rule (around line 88) add the following:

```
#moreTopNews .item {
    margin-right: 5px;
}
```

NOTE: You may remember that **item** is a class we put on all the div tags wrapping our content, so we could style them. It's not special to this plugin.

8. Save the file.

9. Switch to the browser and reload **index.html**. There should now be a little space between the photos.

## An Easy Way to Add Prev & Next Buttons

1. Let's add **next** and **previous** buttons. Switch back to your code editor.

2. Switch to **main.js**.

3. Place your cursor in between the parentheses of **owlCarousel()** and add the following bold code. Don't miss the curly braces {} on the opening and closing lines!

```
$('#moreTopNews').owlCarousel({
    navigation: true
});
```

4. Save the file.

5. Preview **index.html** in a browser and:

   • Try out the **prev** and **next** buttons below the carousel.

   • Notice that each click moves the carousel one item. That requires people to click a lot to view the remaining items, and many won't bother. It should advance to a whole new section of items (however many are currently displayed).

   • While this was an easy way to add them, our design calls for these buttons to be on top of the carousel, to the far right of the **More Top News** line.

6. Switch back to **main.js** in your code editor.

7. Add the following option shown below in bold, and don't miss the comma at the end of the previous line!

```
$('#moreTopNews').owlCarousel({
    navigation: true,
    scrollPerPage: true
});
```

8. Save the file.

9. Switch to the browser and reload **index.html**. Try out the **prev** and **next** buttons again. This time they should move one whole group of items at a time, instead of one at a time. Much better!

## Adding Custom Prev & Next Buttons

The default prev and next buttons are placed below the carousel, but our design calls for them to be above the images (and aligned to the right). For that we'll need to define a custom nav.

1. First we need to code up the buttons. Switch back to your code editor.

2. To save you some typing, we've provided you with the code. From the **snippets** folder, open **carousel-custom-nav.html**.

3. Select and copy all the code.

4. Switch to **index.html**.

5. Around line 33, find the start of the **#moreTopNews** div.

6. Between that and the **h1** above, paste the code. You should end up with:

```
<h1>More Top News</h1>
<div class="customNav">
    <button class="customPrev">Previous</button>
    <button class="customNext">Next</button>
</div>
<div id="moreTopNews" class="owl-carousel">
```

NOTE: Take note of the classes we have added to these elements. These are not special to OWL Carousel (we created them), but we'll need to target them later in our JS code.

7. Notice that we're also using **button** tags, instead of links (the **a** tag). Buttons can be nice when you don't need an href, because the user isn't going anywhere. While **span** or **div** tags could also work, they require us to add CSS to prevent text selection and to add a pointer cursor (as we saw in a previous exercise).

   Our design calls for these elements to look like buttons—with a background color and padding—so the button element works great (although we'll have remove their default border). If we wanted these to look like plain text links though, you'd also have to remove the button's default padding and background color, so in that case you may want to use a link (the **a** tag).

8. Save the file.

9. Switch to **main.js**.

10. The first thing we need to do is remove the original prev/next buttons. Remove the **navigation: true,** line so you end up with the following code:

```
$('#moreTopNews').owlCarousel({
   scrollPerPage: true
});
```

11. To programmatically control this carousel, we need to be able to refer to it. Let's store a reference to it in a variable by adding the following bold code:

**var topNewsCarousel =** $('#moreTopNews').owlCarousel({

12. Now we have to look for when the next and previous buttons are clicked. Add the following bold code:

```
var topNewsCarousel = $("#moreTopNews").owlCarousel({
   scrollPerPage: true
});

$('.customNext').click(function(){

});
$('.customPrev').click(function(){

});

});
```

13. OWL Carousel provides events for next and previous. We can use jQuery's **trigger()** method to trigger those events. Add the following bold code to trigger the appropriate event on our carousel:

```
$('.customNext').click(function(){
   topNewsCarousel.trigger('owl.next');
});
$('.customPrev').click(function(){
   topNewsCarousel.trigger('owl.prev');
});
```

14. Save the file.

15. Switch to the browser and reload **index.html**. Below the **More Top News** heading click the **Previous** and **Next** buttons to see that they work!

16. These are standard HTML buttons that can be placed anywhere, which means you can style them however you like. We have prepared some CSS that will match our page's design. Let's add it now. Switch back to your code editor.

17. From the **snippets** folder, open **custom-nav-styling.css**.

18. Select and copy all the code.

19. Switch to **main.css**.

20. Around line 91, find the **#moreTopNews .item** rule and paste the styles below it.

21. Save the file.

22. Switch to the browser and reload **index.html**. The buttons should now look nicer and be on the far right of the **More Top News** heading line.

---

## Setting How Many Items Are Shown

Currently, the number of items displayed is based on the window/device size. That's awesome for responsive websites. If you want to customize this there are options that allow you to customize how many items are displayed at specific sizes (**itemsDesktop**, **itemsTablet**, **itemsMobile**, etc.). For more info please refer to the demos at **owlgraphic.com/owlcarousel/#demo**

We want our page to always display the same number of items, regardless of window size. To do that, OWL Carousel provides an **itemsCustom** option. We can use this to override the defaults and set exactly how many items are displayed at any window size. This can even be used for responsive sites when you want to define all your own screen sizes.

1. Switch back to your code editor.

2. Switch to **main.js**.

3. Add the **itemsCustom** option (around line 5) as shown below in bold. Don't miss the comma at the end of the previous line!

```
var topNewsCarousel = $('#moreTopNews').owlCarousel({
   scrollPerPage: true,
   itemsCustom: [
      [0, 4]
   ]
});
```

NOTE: The **itemsCustom** option uses square brackets **[ ]** because it's defining an array. Remember that arrays contain a list of values. **[0, 4]** means windows/devices that are **0px** and wider should display **4** items.

In this case we're only giving it one set of values, but it could accept more as shown in the example below. The following code would display 2 items on screens 0px and wider, and 4 items on screens 400px and wider. (Don't actually make this change on this page, it's just an example.)

```
itemsCustom: [
   [0, 2],
   [400, 4]
]
```

4. Save the file.

5. Switch to the browser and reload **index.html**. You should now see 4 items at a time. Resize the window and notice that as desired, it never changes. Great!

6. Switch back to **main.js** in your code editor.

7. Around line 6, change the number of **itemsCustom** from **4** to **3**, as shown below in bold:

```
itemsCustom: [
    [0, 3]
]
```

8. Save the file.

9. Switch to the browser and reload **index.html**. You should now see 3 items at a time.

   NOTE: When working on responsive sites that change the number of items displayed, be careful of your image sizes. Be sure they are made for the widest possible width, so they will only scale down and not up (which can pixelate them).

## Optional Bonus: Lazy Loading Content

Images are typically the largest files in a webpage. They slow down page loading, especially on mobile devices. Currently, all the photos in our carousel are loaded, even if they are not visible! OWL Carousel has an option called lazy loading, which will only load the hidden images if the user clicks the **next** or **previous** button (or swipes, etc. to view additional items). If a user doesn't interact with the carousel, the extra (hidden) images will never be loaded. Let's see how to add lazy loading.

1. Switch to **main.js** in your code editor.

2. Add the following bold code (around line 6) to enable lazy loading:

```
var topNewsCarousel = $('#moreTopNews').owlCarousel({
    scrollPerPage: true,
    lazyLoad: true,
    itemsCustom: [
        [0, 3]
    ]
});
```

3. Save the file.

   There's one more thing we must do. As long as the img tags in our HTML have a **src** attribute, those images will still be downloaded. We need to change this into something HTML won't load, and then OWL Carousel will use JavaScript to load the images intelligently.

4. Switch to **index.html** in your code editor.

5. For every image in the **#moreTopNews** div (which starts around line 37), you must change **src** into **data-src** and add a **lazyOwl** class. Below is an example of what the final code should look like, with the changes shown in bold. Make this same change to all eight images in the **#moreTopNews** div.

```
<img class="lazyOwl" data-src="img/duck.jpg" alt="Ducks. One has a raised leg.">
```

TIP: If your code editor allows you to place multiple cursors, that would come in handy. For example, in Sublime Text you can hold **Cmd** (Mac) or **Ctrl** (Windows) and click to place multiple cursors. Another approach that works in Sublime Text is to highlight the first **img src=** and then hit **Cmd–D** (Mac) or **Ctrl–D** (Windows) to select the following ones (stop after it selects the last one). You can then use your Arrow keys to position the text cursor as needed and make the desired change.

6. Save the file.

7. Preview **index.html** in Chrome. (We'll be using its DevTools.)

8. Hit **Cmd–Opt–J** (Mac) or **Ctrl–Shift–J** (Windows) to bring up the Console.

9. Click on the **Sources** tab.

10. On the left, expand the **img** folder. If you don't see the **img** folder, expand **top**, then go into **file://** and expand the folder inside. Now you should see the **img** folder and can expand it.

11. Notice there is now an **AjaxLoader.gif** (which was included by OWL Carousel).

12. There should only be four **.jpg** files listed (ignore the **.gif** and **.png** files). Three JPEGs are from our carousel, and the fourth JPEG is from our page's header photo.

13. Keeping the DevTools open, scroll down the page so you can see the carousel.

14. While keeping an eye on the list of images, click the carousel's **Next** button. Depending on how fast the images load, you may notice the spinning loader icon appears before the images are loaded.

15. You should see that more images were added to the list! That proves they weren't loaded until required. This way, users will enjoy a faster loading page.

    NOTE: If you want to refer to our final code example, go to **Desktop > Class Files > yourname-JavaScript jQuery Class > Done-Files > Carousel**.

## Exercise Preview

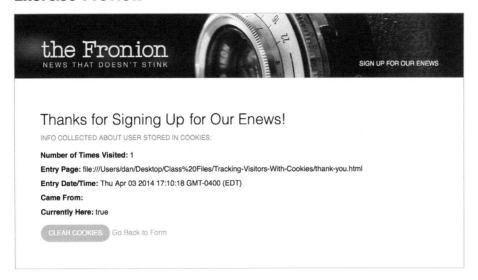

## Exercise Overview

Every website should use analytics to track information about their visitors. That anonymous info is useful, but you can take things a step further if you combine forms with JavaScript—to find users' information such as their landing page, how many times they've visited, where they came from, etc.—and store it in a cookie. When that user submits a form, their info is sent along (invisibly to them), offering you more insight into your customers.

## Previewing Issues to Keep in Mind

Many browsers do not handle cookies consistently when working with local files. They all support cookies on a live site, and all the techniques shown will work fine on a live site. For security and other reasons, cookies at the local level do not always work as expected. Here are some problems we've discovered:

- Internet Explorer on the PC displays an alert bar when using JavaScript locally. This is annoying and does not happen on a live site.

- Older versions of Safari on the Mac sometimes had issues when a parent folder has a space in the name.

- Google Chrome and Microsoft Edge do not display local cookies at all.

  For the above reasons, we will do all previewing in this exercise with **Firefox**.

## Setting Firefox Preferences

Let's make sure Firefox is set up to accept cookies. It is by default, but you or someone else on your computer may have changed the preferences and we want to ensure it works properly for this exercise.

1. Launch **Firefox**.

2. Windows users only: Hit **Alt** to display the menu.

3. Go to **Firefox > Preferences** (Mac) or **Tools > Options** (Windows).

4. Select **Privacy** from the menu.

5. Next to **Firefox will:** choose **Remember history**.

6. Close the window (Mac) or click **OK** (Windows).

---

### Initial Setup Before Moving On

If you are doing this exercise in a classroom (or are doing it for a second time), you must complete the following steps before moving on. If you are doing this exercise at home/work for the first time, you can skip this section.

1. Launch **Firefox**.

2. Hit **Cmd–O** (Mac) or **Ctrl–O** (Windows) to open a file.

3. Navigate to **Desktop > Class Files > yourname-JavaScript jQuery Class** and open the **Tracking-Visitors-With-Cookies** folder.

4. Double–click **set-up.html** to open it.

5. Click the **Clear Cookies** button and then click **OK**. You are done! This has cleared the cookies so you will not be confused by old leftover cookies.

---

## Previewing in Firefox

1. In Firefox, hit **Cmd–O** (Mac) or **Ctrl–O** (Windows) to open a file.

2. Navigate to **Desktop > Class Files > yourname-JavaScript jQuery Class > Tracking-Visitors-With-Cookies**. Find **enews.html** and hit **Open**.

3. This is the page where we'll set some cookies to track user info. Keep this page open in your browser as you work, so you can reload the page to see the changes you make in your code.

## Using a JavaScript API for Handling Cookies

A cookie is a small piece of data that is stored in your browser. Cookies are the easiest way to maintain basic user info and are very versatile—they can perform functions such as tracking your visits to websites, enabling you to log in to sites, and storing your shopping cart. Cookies contain the following information:

- A key-value pair containing the actual data

- An expiry date after which it is no longer valid

- The domain and path of the server it should be sent to

1. Open your code editor if it isn't already open.

2. Close any files you may have open.

3. For this exercise we'll be working with the **Tracking-Visitors-With-Cookies** folder located in **Desktop > Class Files > yourname-JavaScript jQuery Class**. You may want to open that folder in your code editor if it allows you to.

   We'll use **js.cookie.js**, a simple, lightweight JavaScript API (application programming interface) for reading, writing, and deleting cookies developed by Klaus Hartl and Fagner Brack. You can download it and get the documentation from **github.com/js-cookie/js-cookie/**

   NOTE: This API has no dependencies on other JavaScript libraries, so we'll keep our setup as lean as possible by using standard JavaScript instead of loading jQuery.

4. The first order of business is to link to this script. In your code editor, open **enews.html** from the **Tracking-Visitors-With-Cookies** folder.

5. Above the link to main.js (around line 44), add the following bold code:

   ```
   <script src="js/vendor/js.cookie.js"></script>
   <script src="js/main.js"></script>
   ```

6. Save the file.

7. Open **main.js** from the **js** folder in the **Tracking-Visitors-With-Cookies** folder.

8. We want to track how many times a user came to our site before signing up for the newsletter. Create a cookie to store the number of visits by adding this bold code:

   ```
   window.onload = function() {
      Cookies.set( 'visits', 1, {expires: 9000} );
   };
   ```

   NOTE: **Cookies.set()** is a method defined in **js.cookie.js**. This line of code creates a cookie named **visits**. We've set it to a value of **1** because it's their first visit. The cookie will expire in **9000 days**. We'd like to store this cookie for a very long time. If you do not specify the optional expiration time, the cookies will expire when the user quits the browser.

9. Next we'll create a cookie that saves the page they first enter on. JavaScript can look at the current page's href (URL) and save it into a cookie. Add the bold code below:

```
Cookies.set( 'visits', 1, {expires: 9000} );
Cookies.set( 'entryPage', document.location.href, {expires: 9000} );
});
```

10. Now we'll create a cookie that saves the date and time of their first visit. For that, we'll use JavaScript's built-in **Date()** object. Add this bold code:

```
Cookies.set( 'visits', 1, {expires: 9000} );
Cookies.set( 'entryPage', document.location.href, {expires: 9000} );
Cookies.set( 'entryDateTime', Date(), {expires: 9000} );
```

    NOTE: The time will be in 24 hour (military) time with the time zone. The **Date()** object can be reformatted to AM/PM, etc., but the default formatting will suit our needs just fine.

11. Lastly we want to find out the webpage that sent them to the site. JavaScript can get the referring page's href (URL) and save it into a cookie. Add this bold code:

```
Cookies.set( 'visits', 1, {expires: 9000} );
Cookies.set( 'entryPage', document.location.href, {expires: 9000} );
Cookies.set( 'entryDateTime', Date(), {expires: 9000} );
Cookies.set( 'cameFrom', document.referrer, {expires: 9000} );
```

    NOTE: **document.referrer** is the URL of the page the user came from. This will be blank if they directly typed in the URL for the page/site.

12. Save the file.

13. Reload **enews.html** in **Firefox**. As we mentioned earlier in this exercise, other browsers may have problems with local cookies, so be sure to use Firefox.

14. In Firefox, don't fill out the form, just click **Sign Me Up!** to submit it.

15. On the **Thanks for Signing Up** page that appears, check out the values for:

    • **Number of Times Visited**

    • **Entry Page**

    • **Entry Date/Time**

    NOTE: **Came From** will be blank because we are testing locally. You'll have to trust us that it works. We will make the **Currently Here** cookie work later.

16. Find the time part of **Entry Date/Time** and make a note of the time.

17. Click the **Go Back to Form** link (to the right of the **Clear Cookies** button).

18. Click **Sign Me Up!** to submit the form again.

19. Notice that the time changes. Currently, all these cookies are being set every time the user visits the page, but they should only be set on their first visit. Let's fix this.

20. Switch back to **main.js** in your code editor.

21. We need to check to see if the **visits** cookie has been created yet. We can use **Cookies.get()** to do so. If it hasn't, then it is a user's first visit and we should create the cookies. Otherwise, nothing should happen. Add the following bold code:

```
window.onload = function() {
    var v = Cookies.get('visits');
    if ( v == undefined ) {
        Cookies.set( 'visits', 1, {expires: 9000} );
        Cookies.set( 'entryPage', document.location.href, {expires: 9000} );
        Cookies.set( 'entryDateTime', Date(), {expires: 9000} );
        Cookies.set( 'cameFrom', document.referrer, {expires: 9000} );
    }
};
```

NOTE: We're using **v** as a variable name because it's short for **visits**. We already have a **visits** cookie, so we didn't want to use that as a variable name again.

22. Save the file.

23. Switch to Firefox and reload **enews.html**.

24. Click **Sign Me Up!** to submit the form.

Notice that the entry time is still an older time from when you previewed earlier. Hmm. We need to reset our cookies in order to see if the code we wrote is working.

## Clearing Cookies

1. Switch back to your code editor.

2. Open **thank-you.html** from the **Tracking-Visitors-With-Cookies** folder.

3. Let's write some code that will clear out our cookies when we click the **Clear Cookies** button that's on this page. Around line 66, add the following bold code to watch for when our button is clicked:

```
        // Clear Cookies
        document.getElementById('clearCookies').onclick = function() {

        };

    };
</script>
```

4. Next, add the following bold code to clear out our cookies:

```
// Clear Cookies
document.getElementById('clearCookies').onclick = function() {
   Cookies.remove('visits');
   Cookies.remove('entryPage');
   Cookies.remove('entryDateTime');
   Cookies.remove('cameFrom');
   Cookies.remove('currentlyHere');
};
```

5. To make sure our code works, let's get the value of our cookies and write them to the Console so we can see that they've been cleared. Add the following bold code:

```
document.getElementById('clearCookies').onclick = function() {
   Cookies.remove('visits');
   Cookies.remove('entryPage');
   Cookies.remove('entryDateTime');
   Cookies.remove('cameFrom');
   Cookies.remove('currentlyHere');

   console.log(
      Cookies.get('visits'),
      Cookies.get('entryPage'),
      Cookies.get('entryDateTime'),
      Cookies.get('cameFrom'),
      Cookies.get('currentlyHere')
   );
};
```

6. Save the file.

7. Switch to Firefox and reload **enews.html**.

8. Click **Sign Me Up!** to submit the form.

9. Before we clear the cookies, let's open up the Console to make sure it works. **Ctrl–click** (Mac) or **Right–click** (Windows) on the page and select **Inspect Element** to bring up the **Web Developer Tools**.

10. Click the **Console** tab at the top of the Web Developer Tools.

11. Click the **Clear Cookies** button on the page.

12. In the Console, you should see **undefined** 5 times, once for each cookie. This means our cookies have been successfully cleared.

13. Close the Web Developer Tools.

14. Click the **Go Back to Form** link (to the right of the **Clear Cookies** button).

15. Click **Sign Me Up!** to resubmit the form.

    The date should now be just a few seconds old, indicating that the cookies are properly set again.

16. Click the **Go Back to Form** link and then **Sign Me Up!** to submit the form again. Notice that the time does not change. Perfect!

## Updating a Cookie: Incrementing the Number of Visits

1. The **visits** cookie is currently stuck at 1, but it should increment every time the user visits the site. We can increment the value of **v** and then re-save the cookie using the updated value. Return to your code editor.

2. Switch to **main.js**.

3. Add the following bold code:

```
window.onload = function() {
   var v = Cookies.get('visits');
   if ( v == undefined ) {

         ( CODE OMITTED TO SAVE SPACE )

   }
   else {
      v++;
      Cookies.set( 'visits', v, {expires: 9000} );
   }
};
```

    NOTE: **v++** says to take the value of **v** and increment it by 1. Then we set the cookie equal to that new value.

4. Save the file.

5. Return to **thank-you.html** in Firefox and click the **Go Back to Form** link.

6. Click **Sign Me Up!** to submit the form again.

7. Go back and submit the form several times and watch the **Number of Times Visited** increase. (Nothing else should change, just the number of visits.)

    The **visits** cookie should increase every time the user visits the site—but not every time they load a page! We want the visits to increase once per session. (A session ends when the user quits the browser.) This will give a more accurate number of how many times the user has visited your site over time.

8. Return to **main.js** in your code editor.

9. To fix this we will create a cookie called **currentlyHere**. We'll use that to see whether the user is on the site. By not specifying an expiration, it will expire at the end of the session. Add the following bold code:

```
else {
   v++;
   Cookies.set( 'visits', v, {expires: 9000} );
}
Cookies.set( 'currentlyHere', 'true' );
};
```

10. Now let's check to see if the **currentlyHere** cookie exists. If it does not (meaning they have not previously visited the site in this session), we will increase the number of visits. Add the following bold code (there are two places you need to add code):

```
window.onload = function() {
   var v = Cookies.get('visits');
   var c = Cookies.get('currentlyHere');
   if ( v == undefined ) {

      ( CODE OMITTED TO SAVE SPACE )

   }
   else if ( c == undefined ) {
      v++;
      Cookies.set( 'visits', v, {expires: 9000} );
   }
   Cookies.set( 'currentlyHere', 'true' );
};
```

11. Save the file.

12. Return to **thank-you.html** in Firefox.

13. Click the **Go Back to Form** link and then **Sign Me Up!** to submit the form again and:

   • Resubmit the form a few times. Notice that the **Number of Times Visited** does not increase.

   • Stop submitting the form and, on **thank-you.html**, take note of the current **Number of Times Visited**. (You will want to make sure it increases by one in a moment.)

   • Quit Firefox.

   • Preview **enews.html** in Firefox and submit the form again.

   • Notice the **Number of Times Visited** should be one number higher than it was before you quit. This proves our session cookie is working!

## Submitting the Cookie Info with the Form

Our cookies are working, but when a signup form is submitted, it does NOT submit any of the cookie data to the web server. This means the cookie data is only stored on the user's machine and the website owner would never know what it is. We can fix that by creating hidden field inputs in our form. We can then use JavaScript to set the values of those hidden inputs. The values of those hidden inputs can be submitted (along with the rest of the form inputs) so the website owner can see this useful info. Sneaky, huh?

1. Switch back to your code editor.

2. Switch to **enews.html**.

3. We need to create an **input** for each cookie we want to submit along with the form. To save you some typing, we've coded up the HTML. From the **snippets** folder, open **hidden-inputs.html**.

4. Select and copy all the code.

5. Switch back to **enews.html**.

6. Around line 35, find the code for the **Sign Me Up!** submit button.

7. Below that button, paste the code so you end up with the following:

```
<input id="submit" type="submit" name="submit" value="Sign Me Up!">

<input type="text" name="visits" id="visits">
<input type="text" name="entryPage" id="entryPage">
<input type="text" name="entryDateTime" id="entryDateTime">
<input type="text" name="cameFrom" id="cameFrom">
```

NOTE: Notice these are **text** inputs, not **hidden** inputs. As we code we want them to be visible, so we can see their values. When we're done testing, we'll change their type to **hidden**.

8. We need to set the values of these text fields equal to the contents of our cookies. We could add this code to **main.js**, but it's unique to this page. Let's embed it to keep things simple. Add the following bold code before the closing **</body>** tag:

```
<script src="js/main.js"></script>
<script>
   window.onload = function() {

   };
</script>
</body>
</html>
```

9. First let's get the value of the **visits** input. Add the following bold code:

```
<script>
   window.onload = function() {
      document.getElementById('visits').value;
   };
</script>
```

10. Now we can set it to the value of the **visits** cookie. Add the following bold code:

```
window.onload = function() {
   document.getElementById('visits').value = Cookies.get('visits');
};
```

11. We have three other inputs/cookies, so copy and paste that line of code so you end up with a total of **four** lines as shown below. TIP: In Sublime Text you can hit **Cmd–Shift–D** (Mac) or **Ctrl–Shift–D** (Windows) to duplicate the line your cursor is in.

```
window.onload = function() {
   document.getElementById('visits').value = Cookies.get('visits');
   document.getElementById('visits').value = Cookies.get('visits');
   document.getElementById('visits').value = Cookies.get('visits');
   document.getElementById('visits').value = Cookies.get('visits');
};
```

12. We just have to change the names of the form fields and cookies. Make the changes shown in bold:

```
window.onload = function() {
   document.getElementById('visits').value = Cookies.get('visits');
   document.getElementById('entryPage').value = Cookies.get('entryPage');
   document.getElementById('entryDateTime').value =
Cookies.get('entryDateTime');
   document.getElementById('cameFrom').value = Cookies.get('cameFrom');
};
```

13. Save the file.

14. Switch to Firefox, reload **enews.html**, and:

   • Below the **Sign Me Up!** button notice there are some new text fields. These are the ones we just added.

   • The first field should have a number in it. That's the number of visits.

   • The next field should have a URL. That's the entry page.

   • The next field should be the date and time.

   • The last field is empty because there was no referring page, but this would work on a live site.

15. Now that we know they are working, we can change the type from **text** to **hidden** so the user doesn't see these. Return to **enews.html** in your code editor.

16. Find the **input** tags starting around line 37 and change the **type** from **text** to **hidden**. TIP: Sublime Text users can select the first copy of **text**. Then hit **Cmd–D** (Mac) or **Ctrl–D** (Windows) a few times to select the other copies. Once all four are selected, type **hidden** to update them all at once!

```
<input type="hidden" name="visits" id="visits">
<input type="hidden" name="entryPage" id="entryPage">
<input type="hidden" name="entryDateTime" id="entryDateTime">
<input type="hidden" name="cameFrom" id="cameFrom">
```

17. Save the file.

18. Switch to Firefox and reload **enews.html** to see that the fields are hidden. Don't worry though, they still work when hidden!

That's all we have to do for the front-end. You may need to adjust your server-side script that processes the form, so it will include the info from these hidden inputs. The info is there for the taking, though! We hope this lets you gain powerful insights into your web visitors and customers.

NOTE: If you want to refer to our final code example, go to **Desktop > Class Files > yourname-JavaScript jQuery Class > Done-Files > Tracking-Visitors-With-Cookies**.

---

## Exercise Preview

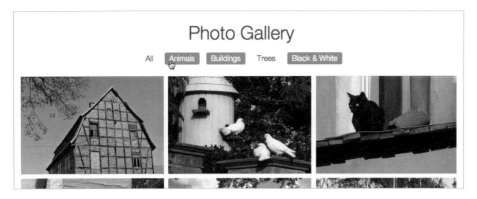

## Exercise Overview

Over the course of the next few exercises, we'll create a filtering system for a photo gallery website. The photographer has taken color and black and white photos of animals, buildings, and trees. By default, all the photos are showing. The ultimate goal is to let the user narrow down the number of images on the page by clicking one or more filter buttons, choosing which image categories they want to see.

In this exercise, we'll create functionality that will allow a user to see when their filter options are selected and deselected. We'll add the functionality for actually filtering the photos in the exercise that follows.

---

## Getting Started

1. Open your code editor if it isn't already open.

2. Close any files you may have open.

3. For this exercise we'll be working with the **Photo-Site-Navigation** folder located in **Desktop > Class Files > yourname-JavaScript jQuery Class**. You may want to open that folder in your code editor if it allows you to (like Sublime Text does).

4. Open **index.html** from the **Photo-Site-Navigation** folder.

5. Preview **index.html** in Chrome (we'll be using its DevTools later).

6. Scroll through the photo gallery to see all the photos displayed. Notice the category links at the top. If you try clicking them, they won't do anything because it's just a static HTML layout. Our job is to write the script to make the navigational user friendly and functional.

   In this exercise, we'll program the navbar so that a user can see whether a filter button is selected or not. We also want to program the All button to visually deselect all the other buttons. We'll make the filter functional in later exercises.

7. Leave the page open in Chrome so we can come back to it later.

## Using Data Attributes to Track User Selection

New in HTML5, you can write custom attributes known as **data attributes** in order to store info and target elements more specifically. This is super helpful because we can avoid creating a bunch of classes or IDs that aren't really meaningful. Data attributes start with **data-** followed by whatever you want to name it.

1. Go back to **index.html** in your code editor.

2. Let's take a look at what we have so far. Locate the navigation around lines 13–21. Notice that the hrefs are only linking to JavaScript. This is because, for this exercise, we'll just be triggering JavaScript with these buttons (not going to URLs).

3. Let's begin by tracking whether a filter choice has been selected or not. We can use data attributes to track this. Add the following bold code:

```
<ul>
   <li><a data-selected="yes" href="javascript:;">All</a></li>
   <li><a data-selected="no" href="javascript:;">Animals</a></li>
   <li><a data-selected="no" href="javascript:;">Buildings</a></li>
   <li><a data-selected="no" href="javascript:;">Trees</a></li>
   <li><a data-selected="no" href="javascript:;">Black &amp; White</a></li>
</ul>
```

NOTE: All of the photos display when the page loads. This is why we want to have the All filter selected by default, while the rest of the filters remain off until a user clicks them.

4. The **All** link will pertain to multiple photo categories, so we want to be able to easily access it. Go ahead and give this link an ID, as shown in bold:

```
<li><a id="all-button" data-selected="yes" href="javascript:;">All</a></li>
```

## Creating Variables to Store the Navigation Items

1. Now it's time to start writing some JavaScript. After the final closing `</div>` tag. Add script tags and a window.onload function, around line 146, as shown:

```
</div>

<script>

   window.onload = function() {

   };

</script>
```

   NOTE: The event handler window.onload waits for all content to be loaded before running any code.

2. We need an easy way to refer to all the links we have in the nav. To do this, let's use **querySelectorAll()** and save them to a variable. With querySelectorAll(), we can use the same exact syntax we use for CSS selectors. querySelectorAll() selects multiple elements and stores them in an array. While we're at it, let's test it in the JavaScript Console. Add the following bold code:

```
window.onload = function() {

   var filterNav = document.querySelectorAll('nav a');
   console.log(filterNav);

};
```

3. Save the file and reload **index.html** in Chrome.

4. Open the Console by hitting **Cmd–Opt–J** (Mac) or **Ctrl–Shift–J** (Windows).

5. Click the **arrow** to the left of the log message if it's not already expanded. You should see the five anchor tags listed. Now we know that the navigation links are being accessed immediately after the window loads—so far, so good!

6. Let's add more functionality. Switch back to your code editor.

7. Around lines 150 and 152, add the following two bold lines of code (you'll need to replace the **console.log()** line of test code with the new var reference):

```
window.onload = function() {

   // grabbing elements
   var filterNav = document.querySelectorAll('nav a');
   var allButton = document.getElementById('all-button');

};
```

NOTE: We will be logically arranging our code by functionality. To help us remember what each section of the code does, we will be adding comments such as this one, which indicated that this is where we'll write all our variable declarations. The new variable saves the all-button so it's easily accessible.

8. Save the file.

## Styling the Selected Buttons

We need to figure out how to keep a button highlighted when it's selected. The highlight on hover function is already coded into our CSS. We can add onto this rule to get the style we want.

1. In your code editor, go to **Photo-Site-Navigation > css** and open **styles.css**.

2. Around line 33, find the **nav a:hover** rule and add another CSS selector as shown below in bold (don't miss the **comma** after hover):

```
nav a:hover,
nav a[data-selected="yes"] {
   color: #fff;
   background: #e07360;
}
```

NOTE: The CSS selector we just added specifies that, once the data-selected attribute is set to **yes**, the link should get white text and a red background.

3. Save the file and reload **index.html** in Chrome. The **All** tab in the nav should already be highlighted in red because its data-selected attribute is set to 'yes' by default.

## Toggling the Filter Buttons

Now that we have our data attributes in place, our elements stored as variables, and the proper CSS style is ready and waiting, we can start writing the functionality! We need to break down our goals into manageable, self-contained tasks and wrap them each in a function.

1. Go back to **index.html** in your code editor and add a new comment around line 154:

```
var allButton = document.getElementById('all-button');
```

### // functions

Let's write our first function. The first task we need to perform is to allow a user to see if they have selected or deselected a category when they click on it. In order to make this work, we need to pass in a **parameter** representing the filter choice the user has made.

2. As shown below in bold, add a function named **toggleCategory(filterChoice)** (filterChoice is the name of the parameter we are passing in):

```
// functions
function toggleCategory(filterChoice) {

    }
};
```

The function needs to toggle the data-selected value. If a category's data-selected value is no (not selected), we need to set it to yes when it's clicked. If it's already set to 'yes', we need to set it to 'no'.

3. Add the following bold conditional that checks the value of the **data-selected** attribute and changes it accordingly:

```
// functions
function toggleCategory(filterChoice) {
    if(filterChoice.getAttribute('data-selected') == 'no') {
        filterChoice.setAttribute('data-selected', 'yes');
    } else {
        filterChoice.setAttribute('data-selected', 'no');
    }
}
```

NOTE: If a category's data-selected value is yes, the CSS rule we wrote earlier will be used to visually highlight the chosen filter option.

4. Now that we've fleshed out the toggleCategory(filterChoice) function, we need to call the function. We'll call it when the user clicks on a filter button. First, we'll need to loop through all the navigation items to find the correct one. Around line 163, add the following bold comment and **for** loop:

```
        filterChoice.setAttribute('data-selected', 'no');
    }
}

// active code
for(var i = 0; i < filterNav.length; i++) {

}
};
```

NOTE: We added the comment to delineate the section of our code that actually executes the functions.

5. When the loop finds the element the user clicked on, we want to change that element's data-selected value. To do that, write the following bold **onclick** function:

```
// active code
for(var i = 0; i < filterNav.length; i++) {
    filterNav[i].onclick = function() {
        toggleCategory(this);
    };
}
```

NOTE: Remember that whenever a function has a parameter, it is asking for information. In order for this kind of function to run correctly, we need to pass arguments to those parameters. We added the keyword **this** as an argument in order to pass in the correct navigation item—the one has been clicked.

6. Save the file.

7. Go to **index.html** in Chrome and reload it.

8. Try clicking on any of the nav buttons and you should see them highlight as they are selected. Click them again to deselect them. Great!

---

## Refining the Filter Buttons

When the All button is selected, none of the other buttons should be highlighted. Likewise, when any of the other buttons are selected, the All category should be deselected. Let's make a function for this.

1. Return to **index.html** in your code editor.

2. Around line 164, above the **//active code** comment, add the bold code shown below:

```
        filterChoice.setAttribute('data-selected', 'no');
    }
}

function deselectOthers(filterChoice) {

}

// active code
```

3. We first need to detect when the All button is being clicked. Earlier, we created a var reference to keep track of this category. Put it to good use by adding the following bold conditional:

```
function deselectOthers(filterChoice) {
    if(filterChoice == allButton) {

    }
}
```

4. The next thing we need to do is loop through the filterNav and deselect all of them except for the All button. Let's start the loop at **1** (instead of 0) to exclude the All button, which is the first one in the array:

```
if(filterChoice == allButton) {
    for(var i = 1; i < filterNav.length; i++) {
        filterNav[i].setAttribute('data-selected', 'no');
    }
}
```

5. Add the following bold **else** statement to specify that the All button should become deselected in the case that any of the other buttons are clicked:

```
function deselectOthers(filterChoice) {
    if(filterChoice == allButton) {
        for(var i = 1; i < filterNav.length; i++) {
            filterNav[i].setAttribute('data-selected', 'no');
        }
    } else {
        allButton.setAttribute('data-selected', 'no');
    }
}
```

Now we need to call this function. But where to do that? Remember, we only want to call this function when the user is setting a filter choice from 'no' to 'yes'. It makes sense to first deselect all the others and then turn on that one selection. Let's call the function at that juncture.

6. Up in the **toggleCategory(filterChoice)** function, around line 154, add the following bold code one line before the data-selected attribute gets changed:

```
// functions
function toggleCategory(filterChoice) {
   if(filterChoice.getAttribute('data-selected') == 'no') {
      deselectOthers(filterChoice);
      filterChoice.setAttribute('data-selected', 'yes');
   } else {
```

7. Save the file and reload **index.html** in Chrome.

8. As before, **All** is selected by default. Click one of the other buttons. The button you clicked should become highlighted, while All becomes deselected.

9. Click another button (besides All) that is not already selected. It should become highlighted along with the one you previously clicked.

10. Click **All** and all the other buttons will deselect.

   Fantastic, we've got the buttons working! In the next exercise, we'll start actually filtering the photos.

   NOTE: If you want to refer to our final code example, go to **Desktop > Class Files > yourname-JavaScript jQuery Class > Done-Files > Photo-Site-Navigation**.

## Exercise Preview

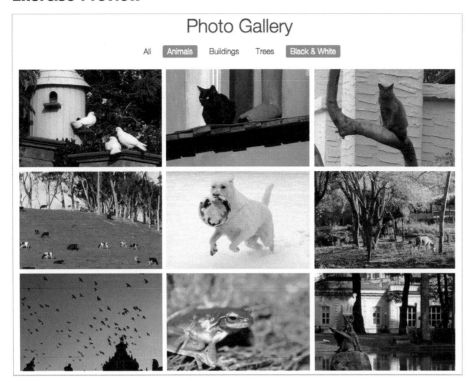

## Exercise Overview

In this exercise, we'll continue building the functionality of the photo gallery website. In the last exercise, we programmed the filter buttons in the navigation to show a user whether a filter is selected or not. Now we'll get them to actually filter the photos.

## Getting Started

1. Open your code editor if it isn't already open.

2. Close any files you may have open.

3. For this exercise we'll be working with the **Photo-Site-Filter** folder located in **Desktop > Class Files > yourname-JavaScript jQuery Class**. You may want to open that folder in your code editor if it allows you to (like Sublime Text does).

4. Open **index.html** from the **Photo-Site-Filter** folder.

5. Preview **index.html** in Chrome (we'll be using its DevTools later).

6. Click the links in the navigation at the top to see that they only look functional. When users click on one or more categories, we want the photos in the main area of the page to actually filter based on their selections.

7. Leave the page open in Chrome so we can come back to it later.

---

## Setting up Data Attributes for Photo Categories

1. Go back to **index.html** in your code editor.

2. Let's take a look at how the images have been categorized in the markup. Starting around line 24, notice that each image is wrapped with a div tag that contains one to four classes that'll assign it to various categories. We can use these classes to make the filter functional.

3. Let's begin by adding data attributes to the navigation items to enable us to store and access the info about what type of photo the user would like to see. Add the following bold code:

```
<ul>
   <li><a data-filter="all" id="all-button" data-selected="yes"
href="javascript:;">All</a></li>
   <li><a data-filter="animals" data-selected="no"
href="javascript:;">Animals</a></li>
   <li><a data-filter="buildings" data-selected="no"
href="javascript:;">Buildings</a></li>
   <li><a data-filter="trees" data-selected="no"
href="javascript:;">Trees</a></li>
   <li><a data-filter="bw" data-selected="no" href="javascript:;">Black &amp;
White</a></li>
</ul>
```

NOTE: The values we've added to the data-attributes here match the classes assigned to the image holders.

---

## Creating an Array to Store the Filter Choices

Bear in mind that there are always numerous ways to program functionality, and what we'll do in this exercise is one of many possible solutions. Breaking down your goals into small, manageable chunks is always a good strategy. Let's add the most basic functionality and work from there.

The first chunk of code we need to write is a function that captures the filter choices and stores them in an array. We will then use the data in the array to filter the photos. To lay the groundwork, let's call the function and declare the array.

1. Switch back to your code editor.

2. In the **active code** that starts around line 174, near the end of the **for** loop, add the following bold code to call the **populateArray()** function we'll add soon:

```
// active code
for(var i = 0; i < filterNav.length; i++) {
    filterNav[i].onclick = function() {
        toggleCategory(this);
        populateArray();
    }
}
```

3. In the **grabbing elements** code that starts around line 150, declare the following bold empty array that'll get populated when the user clicks on a category:

```
// grabbing elements
var filterNav = document.querySelectorAll('nav a');
var allButton = document.getElementById('all-button');
var selectedArray = [];
```

4. Now it's time to write the function itself. At the end of the **functions** section of the code, add the following bold code (around line 175):

```
function populateArray() {

}

// active code
```

5. If a user has already chosen a selector, the array will already be populated. To make sure no info gets duplicated when these users make a new choice, we need to clear out the array every time the function runs. Add this bold code:

```
function populateArray() {
    selectedArray = [];
}
```

---

## Getting the All Button to Show All Filter Values

We need to separate the functionality we're about to code into two different scenarios: either the user will select the All button or the user will select one or more of the other filter buttons, which are much more specific.

# B3  Photo Filter Website: Getting the Photos to Filter

1. Take a look at the markup for the nav, starting around line 15. You should see the following data-filter values:

| Category | Data-Filter Value |
|---|---|
| All | **"all"** |
| Animals | **"animals"** |
| Buildings | **"buildings"** |
| Trees | **"trees"** |
| Black & White | **"bw"** |

   All the data-filter values **except "all"** match a class associated with the gallery content. There are no classes in the markup named all. This means that if the user selects the All button, we'll need to cycle through the data-filter values of the other buttons in the navigation (**animals**, **buildings**, **trees**, and **bw**) in order to create the appropriate array. Otherwise, we want to create an array that only includes the active choices.

2. Around line 177, add the following bold code to the **populateArray()** function:

```
function populateArray() {
   selectedArray = [];
   if(allButton.getAttribute('data-selected') == 'yes') {
      // cycle through every data filter except for 'all'
   } else {
      // get only the active filter choices
   }
}
```

3. To cycle through all the photo categories, we can reference the filterNav variable. If we cycle through starting on 1 instead of 0, we can successfully exclude the all-button, which is the first item. Add the bold loop shown below:

```
if(allButton.getAttribute('data-selected') == 'yes') {
   // cycle through every data filter except for 'all'
   for(var i = 1; i < filterNav.length; i++) {

   }
} else {
   // get only the active filter choices
}
```

4. Now that we're cycling through the navigation items, we want to take the data-filter for each and put it into the selectedArray variable. Use the **push()** method to add these values to the array, as shown in bold:

```
if(allButton.getAttribute('data-selected') == 'yes') {
   // cycle through every data filter except for 'all'
   for(var i = 1; i < filterNav.length; i++) {
      selectedArray.push(filterNav[i].getAttribute('data-filter'));
   }
} else {
```

5. Add a **console.log()** line so we can test how the selectedArray looks so far:

```
for(var i = 1; i < filterNav.length; i++) {
   selectedArray.push(filterNav[i].getAttribute('data-filter'));
}
   console.log(selectedArray);
} else {
```

6. Save the file and reload **index.html** in Chrome.

7. Open the Console by hitting **Cmd–Opt–J** (Mac) or **Ctrl–Shift–J** (Windows).

8. Click the **All** button to deselect the category, then click it again to select it.

   The Console should output **["animals", "buildings", "trees", "bw"]**. Success—all the values for the data-filter attribute have been added to the selectedArray!

9. Leave the Console open in Chrome so we can use it again when we reload the page.

---

## Getting the Rest of the Buttons to Select the Other Filters

1. Switch back to your code editor.

   Now we need to specify what will happen in the **else** condition—where the All category is not selected and one or more of the other buttons are. We still need to cycle through all the options, but we only want to add them to the selectedArray if they have their data-selected attribute set to "yes".

2. In the **else** statement under the comment, add that functionality by typing the following bold code (around line 185):

```
} else {
   // get only the active filter choices
   for(var i = 1; i < filterNav.length; i++) {
      if(filterNav[i].getAttribute('data-selected') == 'yes') {
         selectedArray.push(filterNav[i].getAttribute('data-filter'));
      }
   }
}
```

3. Move the console.log() line from the end of the **if** statement to the area between the end of the conditional and the function (around line 190), as shown:

```
    for(var i = 1; i < filterNav.length; i++) {
        selectedArray.push(filterNav[i].getAttribute('data-filter'));
      }
    } else {
      // get only the active filter choices
      for(var i = 1; i < filterNav.length; i++) {
        if(filterNav[i].getAttribute('data-selected') == 'yes') {
          selectedArray.push(filterNav[i].getAttribute('data-filter'));
        }
      }
    }
    console.log(selectedArray);
}
```

4. Save the file, reload **index.html** in Chrome, and make sure the Console is open.

5. In the nav, click the **Animals** button. In the Console, you should see: ["animals"]

6. Click the **Buildings** category and it should add the buildings selector: ["animals", "buildings"]

7. Click the **Animals** button again to see that only "buildings" remains selected. Great, it's working!

---

## Initially Hiding the Photos

So how are we actually going to get the photos to filter? All the photos are displaying by default when the page loads. They are displayed inline-block, which is helpful because we don't need to worry about collapsing containers when images are removed.

Every time a button is clicked, we want to show/hide images based on the selection. The easiest way to do this is to initially hide all photos when a button is clicked, then show only the ones corresponding to the selected value.

1. Go to **index.html** in your code editor.

2. **Delete** the **console.log()** line around line 190, along with any extra whitespace.

3. Around line 192, declare a function we can use every time we need to hide images:

```
function hideAllPics() {

}

// active code
```

4. We should grab all the image containers and save them to a variable. This will make it easier for us to cycle through all the containers and set them to display: none. At the end of the list of variable declarations (around line 154), add the following:

```
// grabbing elements
var filterNav = document.querySelectorAll('nav a');
var allButton = document.getElementById('all-button');
var selectedArray = [];
var imageContainers = document.querySelectorAll('.gallery div');
```

5. Now that we've created the container variable, we want to cycle through them and hide them. Around line 194, add functionality to the **hideAllPics()** function as shown in bold below:

```
}


function hideAllPics() {
    for(var i = 0; i < imageContainers.length; i++) {
        imageContainers[i].style.display = 'none';
    }
}


// active code
```

6. Just to test that this function is working, temporarily call it around line 204:

```
// active code
for(var i = 0; i < filterNav.length; i++) {
    filterNav[i].onclick = function() {
        toggleCategory(this);
        populateArray();
        hideAllPics();
    }
}
```

7. Save the file.

8. Go to Chrome and reload **index.html**.

9. Click any of the buttons and all the images should disappear. Now we know that this functionality is working, we can write the chunk of code that will display only the photo categories the user chooses.

---

## Getting the Photos to Filter

1. Switch back to your code editor.

2. **Delete** the **hideAllPics();** code around line 204 and make sure to remove any whitespace left over. We'll place it into a new function we'll write next.

# B3 Photo Filter Website: Getting the Photos to Filter

3. At long last, let's write the function for filtering the photos. Around line 199, add:

```
function hideAllPics() {
   for(var i = 0; i < imageContainers.length; i++) {
      imageContainers[i].style.display = 'none';
   }
}

function filterPhotos() {
   hideAllPics();
}

// active code
```

4. Next we want to cycle through the selectedArray and find all the items stored inside it. Add the following bold loop to add that functionality:

```
function filterPhotos() {
   hideAllPics();
   for(var i = 0; i < selectedArray.length; i++) {

   }
}
```

5. Let's create a **group** variable and then use it to store the selected images. Add the following bold lines of code to the **filterPhotos()** function as shown:

```
function filterPhotos() {
   var group;
   hideAllPics();
   for(var i = 0; i < selectedArray.length; i++) {
      group = document.querySelectorAll('.' + selectedArray[i]);
   }
}
```

6. Then we'll take the selected classes from the group and make them display inline-block. Add another loop inside this loop:

```
for(var i = 0; i < selectedArray.length; i++) {
   group = document.querySelectorAll('.' + selectedArray[i]);
   for(var j = 0; j < group.length; j++) {
      group[j].style.display = 'inline-block';
   }
}
```

NOTE: Whenever you're writing a loop within a loop, you can't use the same variable for both. Conventionally, the first loop's variable will be i and the second loop's variable will be j but you could name them whatever you want.

7. Now call the function near the end of the **active code** (around line 216):

```
// active code
for(var i = 0; i < filterNav.length; i++) {
    filterNav[i].onclick = function() {
        toggleCategory(this);
        populateArray();
        filterPhotos();
    }
}
```

8. Save the file.

9. Switch back to Chrome and reload **index.html**.

10. Try clicking the **Black & White** button. Now only black & white photos should be showing!

11. Click the **Animals** button. Now black & white photos as well as photos with animals are showing.

12. Go ahead and click any of the filters on/off. They should all work!

    In summation, this is what's happening: After a selector is toggled, an array is populated. Then the filterPhotos() function fires, which initially hides all photos, goes through the array, sets up queries for everything inside the array, and finally sets the selected images to inline-block.

---

## Optional Bonus: Fixing a Usability Issue

You may have noticed that, if you deselect all the categories and/or toggle the All button off, no photos will be displayed. We'll need to tackle this issue with one final function.

1. Switch back to your code editor.

2. Around line 199, add the following new function that will check to see if we're dealing with an empty array:

```
function hideAllPics() {
    for(var i = 0; i < imageContainers.length; i++) {
        imageContainers[i].style.display = 'none';
    }
}

function noFilterSelection() {
    if(selectedArray == 0) {

    }
}
```

3. If the user deselects all categories and the array is empty, let's just assume they meant to "start again" with all photos showing. Let's loop through the image containers again and set them to display inline-block once more. Add the following bold code:

```
function noFilterSelection() {
   if(selectedArray == 0) {
      for(var i = 0; i < imageContainers.length; i++) {
         imageContainers[i].style.display = 'inline-block';
      }
   }
}
```

4. We can call the new function inside the **filterPhotos()** function. Add the following bold code:

```
function filterPhotos() {
   hideAllPics();
   for(var i = 0; i < selectedArray.length; i++) {
      group = document.querySelectorAll('.' + selectedArray[i]);
      for(var j = 0; j < group.length; j++) {
         group[j].style.display = 'inline-block';
      }
   }
   noFilterSelection();
}
```

5. Save the file.

6. Switch back to Chrome and reload **index.html**, making sure to deselect all filter choices. Better! But we should give the user a visual aid to show they are now seeing All photos once more.

7. Switch back to your code editor.

8. Add the following bold code to the **noFilterSelection()** function:

```
function noFilterSelection() {
   if(selectedArray == 0) {
      for(var i = 0; i < imageContainers.length; i++) {
         imageContainers[i].style.display = 'inline-block';
      }
      allButton.setAttribute('data-selected', 'yes');
   }
}
```

9. Save the file.

10. Switch back to Chrome and reload **index.html**. Super!

    NOTE: If you want to refer to our final code example, go to **Desktop > Class Files > yourname-JavaScript jQuery Class > Done-Files > Photo-Site-Filter**.

    _____

## Exercise Preview

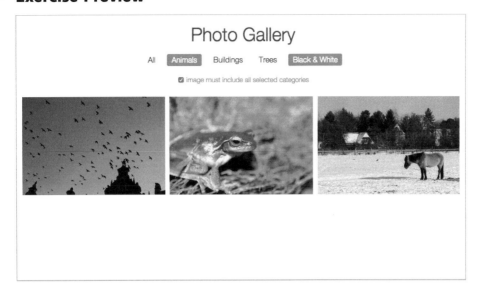

## Exercise Overview

In the previous exercise, we programmed the ability to filter photos on a gallery webpage. The filters we created were additive/inclusive so that when applying multiple filters, they showed photos that matched **any** of the parameters.

In this exercise, we'll learn how to build an exclusive filter feature that will allow a user to show images only if they match all chosen parameters.

## Getting Started

1. Open your code editor if it isn't already open.

2. Close any files you may have open.

3. For this exercise we'll be working with the **Photo-Filter-Exclusive** folder located in **Desktop > Class Files > yourname-JavaScript jQuery Class**. You may want to open that folder in your code editor if it allows you to (like Sublime Text does).

4. Open **index.html** from the **Photo-Filter-Exclusive** folder.

5. Preview **index.html** in Chrome (we'll be using its DevTools later).

6. Click the category links in the navigation at the top to see how the inclusive filtering function selects photos that match any of the selected categories.

7. Leave the page open in Chrome so we can come back to it later.

## Adding a Checkbox to Toggle Exclusive Filtering On/Off

We will be adding an exclusive filtering option via a checkbox that users can click to exclude images if they do not match all selected categories.

1. In order to save time, we've provided the HTML code for the checkbox. Go to **Photo-Filter-Exclusive > snippets** and open **checkbox-toggle.txt**.

2. Check out the code to see that the checkbox includes an ID and label and some text, all contained inside a div. We have already styled these elements for you in the CSS.

3. Select all the code, copy it, and close the file.

4. Back in **index.html**, paste the code before the `</header>` tag (around line 22):

   ```
   </nav>
   <div class="checkbox-toggle">
       <input id="exclusive" name="exclusive" type="checkbox">
       <label for="exclusive">image must include all selected categories</label>
   </div>
   </header>
   <div class="gallery">
   ```

5. Save the file and reload **index.html** in Chrome to see the new checkbox under the nav and before the photos.

## Separating the Inclusive & Exclusive Filters

1. Back in your code editor, find the **filterPhotos()** function that starts around line 212, and **cut** the **var group;** statement and any whitespace.

2. Around line 212, above the filterPhotos() function, create the following bold functions that will separate the filtering into inclusive and exclusive filters (paste the variable into both functions):

   ```
   function filterInclusive() {
      var group;
   }

   function filterExclusive() {
      var group;
   }

   function filterPhotos() {
   ```

3. We coded the logic for the inclusive filter in the previous exercise. This means that all we need to do to flesh out the filterInclusive() function is move some code out of the **filterPhotos()** function. Around lines 222–227, select the **for** loop shown below:

```
for(var i = 0; i < selectedArray.length; i++) {
   group = document.querySelectorAll('.' + selectedArray[i]);
   for(var j = 0; j < group.length; j++) {
      group[j].style.display = 'inline-block';
   }
}
```

4. We can think of this as the **inclusive** for loop. Cut the loop code so we can move it into the inclusive filter.

5. Paste the code inside the **filterInclusive()** function as shown in bold:

```
function filterInclusive() {
   var group;
   for(var i = 0; i < selectedArray.length; i++) {
      group = document.querySelectorAll('.' + selectedArray[i]);
      for(var j = 0; j < group.length; j++) {
         group[j].style.display = 'inline-block';
      }
   }
}
```

## Writing a Conditional to Select the Appropriate Filter

Currently the filterPhotos() function only hides all the photos or shows all the photos if the user deselects all options. Now we need write a conditional that figures out what kind of filter is needed, and provides two directions based on if the checkbox is checked or not. Let's go sleuthing to figure out how to write this conditional statement.

1. The checkbox has an ID of **exclusive** so we'll grab it and store it in a variable. Around line 159, add the following bold code to the end of the variable declarations:

```
var imageContainers = document.querySelectorAll('.gallery div');
var exclusive = document.getElementById('exclusive');

// functions
```

2. Save the file.

3. Go to **index.html** in Chrome and reload it.

4. To determine how to write our conditional, we'll check the checkbox and see what its status is using the handy JavaScript Console. Open the Console by hitting **Cmd–Opt–J** (Mac) or **Ctrl–Shift–J** (Windows).

5. Type the following, then hit **Return** (Mac) or **Enter** (Windows) to look inside the **exclusive** variable we just added (it references the checkbox that toggles the exclusive filter):

```
console.dir(exclusive);
```

6. Click the **arrow** next to **input#exclusive** to expand it.

7. Scroll down to the **checked** value and notice that it is currently **false**.

8. To clear the Console, hit **Cmd–K** (Mac) or **Ctrl–L** (Windows).

9. In the document, check the **checkbox** on under the nav.

10. Type **console.dir(exclusive);** then hit **Return** (Mac) or **Enter** (Windows).

11. Expand **input#exclusive** and scroll to see that **checked** is now **true**.

12. Now that we know that **exclusive.checked** will have a value of either true or false, we can tell the conditional to test for these. Switch back to your code editor.

13. Around line 230, add an **if** statement to the **filterPhotos()** function as shown:

```
function filterPhotos() {
    hideAllPics();
    noFilterSelection();
    if(exclusive.checked) {
        filterExclusive();
    } else {
        filterInclusive();
    }
}
```

NOTE: We could have alternately written line 220 (the first line we added) as if(exclusive.checked **== true**) but we instead wrote a shorthand for saying the same thing. In an if statement the function will only fire if the .checked condition in parentheses is true.

---

### Differentiating the Exclusive Filter

The inclusive filter function is taken care of. Now we need to figure out how to differentiate the exclusive filter. We'll need to place the user's filter choices into the **querySelectAll()** method, but how?

1. Take a look at the following example of the code we might write for the **inclusive** filter if a user selected Animals and Buildings:

```
document.querySelectorAll('.animals');
document.querySelectorAll('.buildings');
```

In the above example, we're grabbing filter values one at a time and adding on to what's already there.

2. In contrast, look at an example of the code for the **exclusive** filter requiring images that contain both Animals and Buildings:

```
document.querySelectorAll('.animals.buildings');
```

In this second example, we're chaining together filter values so both must be present. In order to properly chain the values, we should store them in a string.

3. Before we do anything else, we need a way to be able to access the string for the chained values that will go inside the querySelectorAll() method. In the **filterExclusive()** function, add the following bold variable around line 225:

```
function filterExclusive() {
    var group;
    var queryString = '';
}
```

4. Next we want to loop through the categories the user selected so we can then store this as the value for the string. Add the bold code:

```
function filterExclusive() {
    var group;
    var queryString = '';
    for(var i = 0; i < selectedArray.length; i++) {

    }
}
```

5. Now we'll take queryString and attach the item(s) in the selectedArray. Add:

```
function filterExclusive() {
    var group;
    var queryString = '';
    for(var i = 0; i < selectedArray.length; i++) {
        queryString += '.' + selectedArray[i];
    }
}
```

NOTE: **+=** adds onto the string without deleting what was previously there.

6. We want to make sure our queryString variable is working as intended, so add the bold console.log() line so we can test this in the JavaScript Console:

```
for(var i = 0; i < selectedArray.length; i++) {
    queryString += '.' + selectedArray[i];
}
console.log(queryString);
}
```

7. Save the file.

8. Go to **index.html** in Chrome and reload it.

9. Open the Console if it isn't already open.

10. Check the **checkbox** below the nav.

11. Click the **Animals** button. You should see **.animals** print to the Console.

12. Click the **Buildings** button. You should see **.animals.buildings** print to the Console. It's attaching every filter we select. Perfect!

## Finishing the Exclusive Filter

Next we need to grab the selectors in the queryString, cycle through them, and set them to display inline-block.

1. Back in your code editor, **delete** the console.log() code around line 229.

2. It's a good idea to check whether queryString is empty to be sure it's worth looping through what needs to be displayed. Around line 229, write the bold **if** statement in the case that selectors have been added to the queryString:

```
for(var i = 0; i < selectedArray.length; i++) {
    queryString += '.' + selectedArray[i];
}
if(queryString) {
    group = document.querySelectorAll(queryString);
    for(var j = 0; j < group.length; j++) {
        group[j].style.display = 'inline-block';
    }
}
}
```

NOTE: **if(queryString)** is a simple check to see if queryString is equal to something as opposed to nothing. Additionally, we could have used **i** again as the index variable for the second loop because the first one has already run its course but we use **j** just for clarity here in the second loop.

3. Save the file.

4. Go to **index.html** in Chrome and reload it.

5. Feel free to close the Console if it's open.

6. Right now, all the photos should be showing. Click the **Animals** button.

7. Check the **checkbox** below the nav.

8. Let's filter for just black & white animal photos. Click the **Black & White** button. You should see three results.

9. Click the **All** button and it will show just the one photo that matches all four categories.

10. Try unchecking the checkbox. Hmm, nothing happens because at this point, we haven't programmed it to rerun the filter when the box has been unchecked. We should fix this.

---

## Rerunning the Filter When the Checkbox Is Toggled

We need to specify that whenever the checkbox is checked or unchecked (toggled on or off), we want to populate the array, then filter the photos.

1. Switch back to your code editor.

2. Right under the **// active code** comment, around line 247, add the bold code:

```
// active code
exclusive.onchange = function() {
    populateArray();
    filterPhotos();
}

for(var i = 0; i < selectors.length; i++) {
    selectors[i].onclick = function() {
        toggleSelector(this);
        populateArray();
        filterPhotos();
    }
}
```

3. Save the file.

4. Go to **index.html** in Chrome and reload it.

5. As before, by default, all photos should be showing because it's using the inclusive filter. Check on the **checkbox**.

It should now be showing the one photo that matches all the selectors because it's using the exclusive filter.

6. Uncheck the **checkbox** and watch it go back to using the inclusive filter. Perfect!

   NOTE: If you want to refer to our final code example, go to **Desktop > Class Files > yourname-JavaScript jQuery Class > Done-Files > Photo-Filter-Exclusive**.

---

## Exercise Preview

## Exercise Overview

In the previous exercises we programmed a filtering system for a photo gallery website using standard JavaScript. In this series of two exercises, you'll see how to more quickly and easily recreate this functionality using jQuery. In this first part, we'll work on getting the buttons in the nav to select/deselect. We'll get the photos to filter later.

## Getting Started

1. Open your code editor if it isn't already open.

2. Close any files you may have open.

3. For this exercise we'll be working with the **Photo-Filter-jQuery-1** folder located in **Desktop > Class Files > yourname-JavaScript jQuery Class**. You may want to open that folder in your code editor if it allows you to (like Sublime Text does).

4. Open **gallery-with-js.html** from the **Photo-Filter-jQuery-1** folder. This is the photo gallery filter page that uses standard JavaScript.

5. Open **gallery-with-jquery.html**. This is the photo gallery without any JavaScript added, ready for us to add jQuery.

6. Preview **gallery-with-jquery.html** in Chrome (we'll be using its DevTools later).

7. All the photos show by default and none of the filters work yet. Leave the page open in Chrome so we can come back to it later.

8. Switch back to your code editor.

9. Open **gallery-with-js.html**. As we recreate the filtering system using jQuery, we will use the same logic and structure that we used in the JavaScript version. We'll be referencing this file, but not be editing it.

10. Open **gallery-with-jquery.html**. This is the file we'll be editing.

---

### Adding Variable References: jQuery vs. JavaScript Syntax

1. The first thing we need to do in **gallery-with-jquery.html** is attach jQuery and add script tags where we'll write our custom code. Around line 151, add the bold code:

```
</div>
<script src="js/jquery-2.1.0.min.js"></script>
<script>

</script>
</body>
</html>
```

2. Refer back to **gallery-with-js.html**. Around line 152, we used the window.onload function.

3. There is a better way to do this in jQuery. In **gallery-with-jquery.html**, on line 153, add jQuery's document ready code. Sublime Text Users can type **r** to bring up the **$ (document).ready** snippet, then hit **Return** (Mac) or **Enter** (Windows):

```
<script src="js/jquery-2.1.0.min.js"></script>
<script>
    $(document).ready(function() {

    });
</script>
```

4. Back in **gallery-with-js.html**, look around line 154 to find the **// grabbing elements** comment. The first thing we want to do is grab the navigation items and save them to variables.

5. A common practice whenever you're saving a jQuery object to a variable is to put a **$** in front of the variable name so you can tell it apart from non-jQuery variables. Return to **gallery-with-jquery.html** around line 155, declare a jQuery variable:

```
<script>
    $(document).ready(function() {

        var $filterNav = $('nav a'),

    });
</script>
```

6. Next we want to grab the **all-button**. Add the bold code:

```
$(document).ready(function() {

   var $filterNav = $('nav a'),
       $allButton = $('#all-button'),

});
```

NOTE: We are grouping multiple variable declarations into one statement. These declarations are comma-delineated. The semi-colon is reserved for the last one. You can reference **gallery-with-js.html** to see what we'll be grabbing next.

7. The next variable (selectedArray) we're going to declare is actually not a jQuery object, so we'll just write it as JavaScript. Add:

```
$(document).ready(function() {

   var $filterNav = $('nav a'),
       $allButton = $('#all-button'),
       selectedArray = [],

});
```

8. Add two remaining vars: the imageContainers, and the exclusive filter checkbox:

```
$(document).ready(function() {

   var $filterNav = $('nav a'),
       $allButton = $('#all-button'),
       selectedArray = [],
       $imageContainers = $('.gallery div'),
       $exclusive = $('#exclusive');

});
```

## Attaching a Click Event Handler Using the On() Method

1. In **gallery-with-js.html**, scroll to the active code section and around line 253, locate the **for loop**. At this point, we cycled through all of the navigation items and added an onclick method to each of them. To accomplish this in JavaScript, we had to loop through them all, add onclick and assign a function.

   In jQuery, it's much easier. If you are going to add a method that exists in jQuery onto a group of elements, it will do it automatically in the background without having to cycle through an explicit loop.

2. In **gallery-with-jquery.html**, around line 161, add the following click() method and message that we will test in the JavaScript Console:

```
$(document).ready(function() {

    ( FIVE VARS OMITTED TO SAVE SPACE )

        $exclusive = $('#exclusive');

    $filterNav.click(function() {
        console.log('clicked');
    });

});
```

3. Save the file.

4. Go to Chrome where you should still have **gallery-with-jquery.html** open. Reload it.

5. **Cmd–Opt–J** (Mac) or **Ctrl–Shift–J** (Windows) to bring up the Console.

6. Click any of the buttons in the nav. You should see it say **clicked** in the Console.

   Using the click() method in jQuery is perfectly fine, however, there is a slightly better practice in jQuery whenever you're attaching event handlers like this: using the **on()** method and passing in the value for the kind of event you want to use.

7. Open a separate browser tab or window and navigate to: **api.jquery.com**

8. In the search bar at the upper right of the page, search for: **.on()**

9. In the results below, click: **.on()**

10. Scroll down under **Direct and delegated events** and find the code shown below.

```
1  $( "#dataTable tbody tr" ).on( "click", function() {
2    console.log( $( this ).text() );
3  });
```

    If you want to attach something with **click**, this is an example of how you'd write it. Likewise, you could replace click with **change** or **hover** or **focus**, etc. The value of doing this is that if you want to attach multiple actions on that click, you can do that in multiple different places. For example, you could specify this element does one thing on click, and then later on in your code you could specify that it also does another thing on click. They will be combined together into one. On the other hand, if you just used .click() it would override everything.

11. Switch back to your code editor.

12. Around line 161, replace **click(function()** with the following bold code:

```
$filterNav.on('click', function() {
    console.log('clicked');
});
```

13. Save the file.

14. Go to Chrome and reload **gallery-with-jquery.html**.

15. Open the Console if it isn't already.

16. Click the buttons in the nav to see that they still print **clicked** to the Console.

---

## Toggling the Filter Buttons Using jQuery

1. Switch back to your code editor.

2. **Delete** the **console.log('clicked');** code around line 162.

3. Let's see the standard JavaScript version of the code that'll replace console.log(). In **gallery-with-js.html** around line 255, notice the code: toggleCategory(this);

   The next thing we want to do is call the toggleCategory(filterChoice) function that was declared around line 164. This will highlight/unhighlight a filter button when it is clicked. The syntax will be slightly different in the jQuery version because we are working in the jQuery object.

4. In **gallery-with-jquery.html** within the **on()** method, add the following bold code around line 162:

   ```
   $filterNav.on('click', function() {
       toggleCategory($(this));
   });
   ```

   NOTE: Remember that we're calling **$**(this) because we're working inside the jQuery object.

5. Around line 161, write the function for toggleCategory(filterChoice):

   ```
       $exclusive = $('#exclusive');

   function toggleCategory(filterChoice) {

   }

   $filterNav.on('click', function() {
       toggleCategory($(this));
   });
   ```

6. Let's see how we coded the standard JavaScript version of this function. In **gallery-with-js.html** in the toggleCategory(filterChoice) function, find the conditional statement around lines 163–168.

   We want to set the data-selected attribute to either 'yes' or 'no'. The jQuery code will be similar but more terse.

7. In **gallery-with-jquery.html** add the following bold **if** statement:

```
function toggleCategory(filterChoice) {
   if(filterChoice.attr('data-selected') == 'no') {
      filterChoice.attr('data-selected', 'yes');
   } else {
      filterChoice.attr('data-selected', 'no');
   }
}
```

8. Save the file, switch to Chrome, and reload **gallery-with-jquery.html**.

9. Select, then deselect any of the nav buttons to see that the function is working.

___

## The All Button vs. the Rest of the Buttons

1. Next we want to make it so that when the All category is selected, none of the other buttons are highlighted. Likewise, if Animals, Buildings, Trees, or Black & White are selected, the All button should not be. Switch back to your code editor.

2. In **gallery-with-js.html** around line 164, find the **deselectOthers(filterChoice);** line of code. First, when a filter button is clicked, we need to deselect others.

3. In **gallery-with-jquery.html** around line 163, add the code as shown:

```
function toggleCategory(filterChoice) {
   if(filterChoice.attr('data-selected') == 'no') {
      deselectOthers(filterChoice);
      filterChoice.attr('data-selected', 'yes');
   } else {
      filterChoice.attr('data-selected', 'no');
   }
}
```

4. Now we need to write the function for deselecting others. Look at **gallery-with-js.html** starting around line 171 to see the function we originally wrote.

5. In **gallery-with-jquery.html** around line 170, add the function as shown:

```
function toggleCategory(filterChoice) {

   ( CODE OMITTED TO SAVE SPACE )

}


function deselectOthers(filterChoice) {

}


$filterNav.on('click', function() {
```

6. We need to determine if the All button is selected or not. In JavaScript we used filterChoice == allButton but in jQuery we'll use the .is() method. Add the following **if** statement:

```
function deselectOthers(filterChoice) {
   if(filterChoice.is($allButton)) {
      console.log('yes');
   } else {
      console.log('no');
   }
}
```

7. Save the file, switch to Chrome, and reload **gallery-with-jquery.html**.

8. Open the Console if it isn't already.

9. Click any of the nav filter buttons (besides the All button) and you should see **no** print to the Console.

10. Click the **All** button to deselect it, then click it again to select it. You should see **yes** print to the Console. Now we know the function is properly detecting if All is selected or not.

11. Switch back to your code editor.

12. Look at **gallery-with-js.html** around lines 173–175 to find the **for loop**. Though we had to write a for loop in JavaScript, luckily we won't need to rewrite that loop version because jQuery will take care of that for us. Instead all we need to do is grab all the navigation items and set data-selected to no.

13. In **gallery-with-jquery.html** around line 172, replace **console.log('yes');** with:

```
function deselectOthers(filterChoice) {
   if(filterChoice.is($allButton)) {
      $filterNav.attr('data-selected', 'no');
   } else {
      console.log('no');
   }
}
```

14. In the case that the All button isn't selected, we need to turn it off. Around line 174, replace **console.log('no');** with:

```
function deselectOthers(filterChoice) {
   if(filterChoice.is($allButton)) {
      $filterNav.attr('data-selected', 'no');
   } else {
      $allButton.attr('data-selected', 'no');
   }
}
```

15. Save the file, switch to Chrome, and reload **gallery-with-jquery.html**.

16. Notice the **All** button is still selected by default. Click any of the other buttons and it turns off.

17. Click the **All** button and the other buttons become deselected. That's exactly what we want.

18. Leave the files open in your code editor so you can continue working on them in the next exercise.

    NOTE: If you want to refer to our final code example, go to **Desktop > Class Files > yourname-JavaScript jQuery Class > Done-Files > Photo-Filter-jQuery-1**.

## Exercise Preview

## Exercise Overview

In this exercise, we'll continue where the previous exercise left off, creating the photo gallery using jQuery. In the last exercise, we got the buttons in the nav to select/deselect when clicked. In this exercise, we'll write the code to filter the photos.

1. If you completed the previous exercise, **gallery-with-jquery.html** and **gallery-with-js.html** should still be open in your code editor, and you can skip the following sidebar. We recommend you finish the previous exercise (B5) before starting this one. If you haven't finished it, do the following sidebar.

> **If You Did Not Do the Previous Exercise (B5)**
>
> 1. Close any files you may have open.
>
> 2. Go into **Desktop > Class Files > yourname-JavaScript jQuery Class** and open the **Photo-Filter-jQuery-2** folder.
>
> 3. Open **gallery-with-jquery.html**. This is the photo gallery that we'll be editing with jQuery.
>
> 4. Also open **gallery-with-js.html** from the **Photo-Filter-jQuery-2** folder. This is the photo gallery that we completed in exercise 3D using JavaScript. We'll use this as a reference.

## Populating a Standard JavaScript Array Using jQuery

In the last exercise, we got the navigation elements working. We also created an empty array to store the selected photo data-filter attributes. Next we need to populate the array by cycling through, grabbing the data-filter attributes of each element, and putting the selected items into the array.

1. To see which function we used to populate the array with standard JavaScript, go to **gallery-with-js.html** in your code editor and look around line 256.

2. Switch to **gallery-with-jquery.html**. Around line 180, call the populateArray() function as shown in bold:

```
$filterNav.on('click', function() {
    toggleCategory($(this));
    populateArray();
});
```

3. Refer back to **gallery-with-js.html** around lines 181–196 to check out the standard JavaScript version of the populateArray() function.

4. In **gallery-with-jquery.html** around line 178, add the function as shown in bold:

```
function deselectOthers(filterChoice) {

    ( CODE OMITTED TO SAVE SPACE )

}


function populateArray() {


}


$filterNav.on('click', function() {
```

5. The first thing we need to do in the populateArray() function is take the selected array and reset it back to an empty array. Add same JavaScript code as before:

```
function populateArray() {
    selectedArray = [];
}
```

6. Add an conditional statement to check if the All button is selected:

```
function populateArray() {
    selectedArray = [];
    if($allButton.attr('data-selected') == 'yes') {

    } else {

    }
}
```

7.  Next we want to go through every filter except for **all**, take their data-filter values, and push them onto the selected array. To see how we did this using standard JavaScript, go to **gallery-with-js.html** and find the **for** loop around lines 185–187.

    Earlier in the workbook, you learned that if you want to use a jQuery method such as click() to apply something to everything in a group of elements (e.g. all the buttons in the navigation), you don't need to write a loop because jQuery automatically performs a implicit loop over all of the matched elements.

    Because selectedArray is not a jQuery object, we have to use a different approach. We can use the handy jQuery **.each()** method. You can think of this **explicit loop** as a less complicated version of JavaScript's **for** loop.

8.  Add the **each** method inside the **if** statement around line 181 and also add a console.log() line (around line 187), so we can see exactly what the selectedArray looks like at this point:

```
function populateArray() {
    selectedArray = [];
    if($allButton.attr('data-selected') == 'yes') {
        $filterNav.each(function() {
            selectedArray.push($(this).attr('data-filter'));
        });
    } else {

    }
    console.log(selectedArray);
}
```

9.  Save the file.

10. Preview **index.html** in Chrome to see what we have so far (we'll use its DevTools).

11. Open the Console by hitting **Cmd–Opt–J** (Mac) or **Ctrl–Shift–J** (Windows).

12. Click the **All** button in the nav to deselect it. You should see **[]** print to the Console, indicating an empty array.

13. Click the **All** button again to select it. In the Console, you should see all the filter values in the array: **["all", "animals", "buildings", "trees", "bw"]**

## Using JavaScript to Skip Over the Zero Index

The only problem is it also grabbed "all" which we don't want because we don't have an all class we can apply. How do we get rid of it? This is an example of the limitations of trying to use just jQuery; sometimes when you want to do something more advanced you'll also need to use JavaScript.

1.  Leave **gallery-with-jquery.html** open in Chrome so we can come back to it later.

2. Return to your code editor.

3. In **gallery-with-jquery.html** look at the code inside the each() method around line 182 to see that it's going through the entire array and grabbing all the filter choices. We don't have a way to skip over the 0 index (which would be the first item)!

4. Let's try using the native JavaScript **shift()** method to skip over the All selector and shift the other values. Around line 185, add the following bold code:

```
if($allButton.attr('data-selected') == 'yes') {
   $filterNav.each(function() {
      selectedArray.push($(this).attr('data-filter'));
   });
   selectedArray.shift();
} else {
```

NOTE: The **shift()** method deletes the first item in the Array and "shifts" the other values so that 1 becomes 0, 2 becomes 1, etc.

5. Save the file.

6. Go to Chrome and reload **gallery-with-jquery.html**.

7. Open the Console if it's not already open.

8. Click the **All** button in the nav to deselect it. As before, you should see **[]** print to the Console, indicating an empty array.

9. Click the **All** button again to select it. In the Console, you should see all the array's filter values, minus "all": **["animals", "buildings", "trees", "bw"]**

## Selecting Buttons Other than the All Button

In the case that a user clicks on any filter button other than the All selector, we want to run through the filters again, but this time we only want to push to the array if the data-selected attribute is set to "yes".

1. Return to your code editor.

2. Add the following bold code inside the **else** statement starting around line 186:

```
} else {
   $filterNav.each(function() {
      if($(this).attr('data-selected') == 'yes') {
         selectedArray.push($(this).attr('data-filter'));
      }
   });
}
console.log(selectedArray);
```

3. Save the file.

4. Go to Chrome and reload **gallery-with-jquery.html**.

5. Open the Console if it's not already open.

6. Click any of the filter buttons besides All and you should see the filter values appear in the Console. Great, the array is being populated successfully!

## Hiding the Photos

1. Switch back to your code editor.

2. Still in **gallery-with-jquery.html**, call the filterPhotos() function around line 198:

```
$filterNav.on('click', function() {
    toggleSelector($(this));
    populateArray();
    filterPhotos();
});
```

3. Around line 192, **delete** the **console.log(selectedArray);** line as well as any leftover whitespace.

4. Around line 194, declare the filterPhotos() function as shown in bold:

```
}

function filterPhotos() {

}

$filterNav.on('click', function() {
```

5. Refer back to **gallery-with-js.html** (around line 237 near the beginning of the filterPhotos() function) to see that the first thing we did in this function was hide all the photos.

6. First let's call the function to hide the photos. Back in **gallery-with-jquery.html**, add the following code in bold:

```
function filterPhotos() {
    hideAllPics();
}
```

7. We need to declare this actual function. Above the filterPhotos() function, around line 194, add the following code in bold:

```
function hideAllPics() {

}

function filterPhotos() {
```

8. In **gallery-with-js.html**, look around lines 199–202 to see that the hideAllPics() function contains a loop that says to take all the imageContainers (the divs with the gallery class) and set them to display = 'none'.

9. Because we are referencing these divs using jQuery, we can simply use either jQuery's **hide()** or **css()** method and jQuery will perform an implicit loop. In **gallery-with-jquery.html** around line 195, add the bold code shown below:

```
function hideAllPics() {
    $imageContainers.hide();
}
```

NOTE: Instead of .hide(); we could have used .css('display', 'none');

10. Save the file.

11. Go to Chrome and reload **gallery-with-jquery.html**.

12. Click any of the filter buttons and you should see all the images disappear… It's working so far!

---

## Testing the Checkbox's Functionality

Next we need to get the checkbox to filter exclusively (if checked) or filter inclusively (if not checked). Let's test the functionality in the JavaScript Console.

1. Switch back to your code editor.

2. In the filterPhotos() function, add the following bold code around line 200:

```
function filterPhotos() {
    hideAllPics();
    if($exclusive.is(':checked')) {
        console.log('checked');
    } else {
        console.log('not checked');
    }
}
```

NOTE: :checked is a pseudo-class, like :hover.

3. Save the file.

4. Let's test if this is working. Go to Chrome and reload the page.

5. Make sure the Console is open.

6. Click one of the filter buttons and you should see **not checked** print to the Console because the checkbox is not checked by default.

7. Check on the **checkbox**, then click one of the filter buttons. You should see **checked** print to the Console. Cool, it's working as expected!

# B6

## Programming the Inclusive Filter

Let's start by creating the inclusive filter (for searches that include any filter).

1. Back in your code editor, **delete** the **console.log()**s around lines 207 and 209.

2. In the **else** statement around line 209, call the function we're about to write:

```
function filterPhotos() {
    hideAllPics();
    if($exclusive.is(':checked')) {

    } else {
        filterInclusive();
    }
}
```

3. Declare the actual function around line 198, between the hideAllPics() and filterPhotos() functions:

```
}

function filterInclusive() {

}

function filterPhotos() {
```

4. Look back at **gallery-with-js.html** to check out the filterInclusive() function around lines 213–221. This is what we did:

   • First we created a variable called **group**.

   • Then we cycled through the **selectedArray** using a **for** loop.

   • If the condition is met, JavaScript takes everything inside the **selectedArray**, attaches a **'.'** to make it a class, puts it into the **querySelectorAll()** method, and saves that to the **group** variable.

   • Finally, the other loop sets the group's **display** property to **inline-block**.

5. We need to run through the values in the selectedArray and apply a function to them. It sounds like it would make sense to use the .each() method, but it won't work as expected. In **gallery-with-jquery.html**, add the bold code around line 199 to see what happens:

```
function filterInclusive() {
    selectedArray.each(function() {
        console.log('hello');
    });
}
```

6. Save the file.

7. Go to Chrome and reload the page.

8. Make sure the Console is open, then click on a filter button in the nav. In the Console, you'll see an error: **selectedArray.each is not a function**.

   The problem is that selectedArray is not a jQuery object. While we normally can't call jQuery functions on non-jQuery objects, there is a way around this.

9. Let's figure this out. In a new browser tab or window, go to: **api.jquery.com**

10. In the search bar towards the top right, search for: **$.each**

11. In the results, click on **jQuery.each()** (this is the same as $.each()—remember that $ is an alias for jQuery).

    This function allows you to call jQuery and attach a non-jQuery **array** as the first argument. For the second argument, you put the **callback** or function you want to apply to the array.

12. Switch back to your code editor.

13. **Delete** the **selectedArray.each()** function (around lines 199–201):

```
selectedArray.each(function() {
    console.log('hello');
});
```

14. We want to pass in a function that we'll apply to each item in the array. Replace the deleted code with the jQuery.each() method that includes multiple arguments:

```
function filterInclusive() {
    $.each(selectedArray, function(i) {

    });
}
```

    NOTE: The function takes a counter variable called **i** as an argument. We are passing it in as an index for whatever we're cycling through in the selectedArray.

15. Around line 200, add the following bold code:

```
function filterInclusive() {
    $.each(selectedArray, function(i) {
        $('.' + selectedArray[i]).show();
    });
}
```

    NOTE: We're using the jQuery .each() method to pass in the selectedArray (a non-jQuery object) and perform the function on it (where we'll be using the index of whatever we're cycling through). Then we add the '.' to add a class selector onto the results, add the selectedArray value, and show the appropriate photos.

16. Save the file.

17. Go to Chrome and reload the page.

18. Click the **Black & White** button (you could click any, but it's easiest to spot the effect). You should see just the black and white photos filter.

19. Click **Trees** and you'll see photos that are either black & white OR have trees.

## Programming the Exclusive Filter

1. Switch back to your code editor.

2. In the filterPhotos() function, around line 204, specify the following bold functionality that will run if the $exclusive checkbox is checked:

```
function filterPhotos() {
    hideAllPics();
    if($exclusive.is(':checked')) {
        filterExclusive();
    } else {
        filterInclusive();
    }
}
```

3. Around line 204, between the filterInclusive() and filterPhotos() functions, declare the **filterExclusive()** function as shown in bold:

```
}

function filterExclusive() {

}

function filterPhotos() {
```

4. Look back at **gallery-with-js.html** to check out the filterExclusive() function around lines 223–235 to see what we did in the standard JavaScript version.

   We put together a queryString and cycled through everything in the array. Then we took everything out of the array and added it to the queryString. Once we had a queryString (that wasn't empty), we set it to display inline-block. Fortunately, jQuery's going to help us simply this significantly.

5. Back in **gallery-with-jquery.html**, around line 205, declare the queryString variable and set it to be an empty string:

```
function filterExclusive() {
    var queryString = '';
}
```

6. We need to cycle through the array and add it to the queryString. To do that, we'll use the .each() method again. Around line 206, add:

```
function filterExclusive() {
   var queryString = '';
   $.each(selectedArray, function(i) {
      queryString += ('.' + selectedArray[i]);
   });
   console.log(queryString);
}
```

7. Save the file.

8. Go to Chrome and reload the page. Make sure the Console is open.

9. Check on the **checkbox** under the nav.

10. Click the **Trees** button. You should see **.trees** print to the Console.

11. Click the **Buildings** button. You should see **.buildings.trees** print to the Console.

12. Click the **All** button and you'll see **.animals.buildings.trees.bw** print to the Console. Great, the correct classes are being selected.

13. Back in your code editor, around line 209, replace **console.log(queryString);** with the following bold **if** statement:

```
function filterExclusive() {
   var queryString = '';
   $.each(selectedArray, function(i) {
      queryString += ('.' + selectedArray[i]);
   });
   if(queryString) {
      $(queryString).show();
   }
}
```

14. Save the file, go to Chrome, and reload the page.

15. Check on the **checkbox** under the nav.

16. Click the **Animals** and **Black & White** buttons. Now only black & white photos with animals are showing!

---

## Rerunning the Filter When the Checkbox Is Toggled

1. Now we need to specify what will happen whenever the checkbox is checked or unchecked (toggled on or off). The process will be pretty similar to how we did it with JavaScript. Return to **gallery-with-jquery.html** in your code editor.

2. Below the end of the filterPhotos() function, around line 223, add:

```
}

$exclusive.on('change', function() {
    populateArray();
    filterPhotos();
});

$filterNav.on('click', function() {
```

3. Save the file, go to Chrome, and reload the page.

4. Click any two filter buttons in the nav.

5. Check on the **checkbox**. Exclusive filtering should turn on.

6. Uncheck the **checkbox**. It should start inclusive filtering.

## Improving the User Experience

The finished photo filter page works wonderfully unless a user deselects all buttons. Let's fix this.

1. Switch back to your code editor.

2. We'll need to create a function that will address the issue. Around line 223, add the following function:

```
}

function noFilterSelection() {

}

$exclusive.on('change', function() {
```

3. All we need to do is check to see if selectedArray is empty. If it's empty, we can just assume they meant to "start again" with all the photos showing:

```
function noFilterSelection() {
    if(selectedArray.length == 0) {
      $imageContainers.show();
    }
}
```

4. We will also want the **All** button to highlight, to let the users know what's going on. Add the following:

```
function noFilterSelection() {
    if(selectedArray.length == 0) {
        $imageContainers.show();
        $allButton.attr('data-selected', 'yes');
    }
}
```

5. Finally, we'll need to call this function. Around line 216, call the function inside the **filterPhotos()** function, as follows:

```
function filterPhotos() {
    hideAllPics();
    noFilterSelection();
    if($exclusive.is(':checked')) {
        filterExclusive();
    } else {
        filterInclusive();
    }
}
```

6. Save the file.

7. Return to **gallery-with-jquery.html** in Chrome and reload the page. Deselect all filter buttons. Perfect!

So in summary, we were able to redo the photo gallery in jQuery and it was simpler and faster and required less code.

NOTE: If you want to refer to our final code example, go to **Desktop > Class Files > yourname-JavaScript jQuery Class > Done-Files > Photo-Filter-jQuery-2**.

# Check Out
# OUR OTHER WORKBOOKS!

Web Development
Level 1 and 2

JavaScript & jQuery

GreenSock Animation

Mobile & Responsive
Web Design

WordPress

PHP & MySQL

Ruby on Rails

Photoshop for Web & UI

Photoshop Animated GIFs

Adobe Experience Design

Sketch

HTML Email

Responsive HTML Email

PowerPoint

Adobe InDesign

Adobe Illustrator

Adobe Photoshop

Photoshop Advanced

Adobe Lightroom

Adobe After Effects

Adobe CC: Intro to InDesign,
Photoshop, & Illustrator

## NOBLEDESKTOP.COM/BOOKS

# Websites for Scripts & Plugins

---

## jQuery Plugins

Below is a list of websites for the scripts taught in this workbook. We wanted to make them easier to find, so you don't have to search for them in the workbook. Happy coding!

- **jQuery**
  jquery.com

- **Magnific Popup Plugin**
  dimsemenov.com/plugins/magnific-popup

- **Cycle Plugin**
  malsup.com/jquery/cycle2

- **OWL Carousel Plugin**
  owlgraphic.com/owlcarousel

- **Form Validation Plugin**
  jqueryvalidation.org

- **Cookies Plugin**
  github.com/js-cookie/js-cookie

---

## JavaScript Resources

These aren't used in the book, but they are still good sites to know about anyway!

- **Online JavaScript/CSS Compressor** (Requires proper semi-colon use. Use either **JSLint** or **JSHint** to detect missing semi-colons.)
  refresh-sf.com

- **JSLint: Douglas Crockford's JavaScript Code Quality Tool**
  jslint.com

- **JSHint: JavaScript Code Quality Tool** (can be less strict than JSLint)
  jshint.com

---

# Common JavaScript Terms Defined

Here's a concise list of common JavaScript terms/concepts and their definitions.

- **Arguments vs. Parameters**:
  When defining a function, you can request information to be passed to it (so you can use it in the function). When defining a function, it's written as:
  ```
  function myFunctionName(parameter1,parameter2)
  ```

  Later when calling the function, you pass **arguments** to those **parameters** as:
  ```
  myFunctionName(argument1,argument2)
  ```

- **Array**:
  Like an object, it's a collection of things such as strings, numbers, booleans, functions, objects, or other arrays. Unlike an object, you don't get to name the keys. Keys are numbered automatically in ascending order starting from 0.

- **Concatenation**:
  Putting strings together is called concatenation. The strings are put together, one after the other, for instance: `string1 + string2 = string1string2`

- **Function**:
  Defines a group of code. This code is not executed until it is called.

- **jQuery**:
  A free JavaScript framework (pre-written JavaScript) widely used in web development. There are many plugins developed around the jQuery library.

- **Key-Value Pair**:
  How objects are typically organized. Key-value pairs have a **key** (attribute) followed by a **colon** and the **value** associated with the key. You can name a key anything as long as it doesn't start with a number. Multiple key-value pairs are comma-delimited except for the last one. As shown in the bold key-value pairs below, you can assign any type of value to a key, such as strings, numbers, and booleans:
  ```
  var myObject = {
      name: 'Bob',
      age: 23,
      alive: true
  }
  ```

- **Loop**:
  A chunk of code that is used for quickly repeating a task many times in a row. The for loop is the most common. It takes three pieces of information in this order: a **counter** variable (usually named i), a **condition** to test, and an **incrementer**. If the condition is true, the instructions in curly braces will execute every time the loop runs. The syntax is shown below:
  ```
  for (counter; condition; incrementer) {
      // Code to execute if the condition is true
  }
  ```

# Common JavaScript Terms Defined

- **Method**:
These are like the verbs of JavaScript. They are built-in actions that do various tasks. They are written as: `methodName()`.

- **Object**:
A bundle of information that is packaged in an organized way and has key-value pairs that you write. Nearly everything in JavaScript is an object. You can name an object anything as long as it doesn't start with a number.

- **Property**:
Objects have properties. These are like the adjectives of JavaScript. They tell you things about an object. You can get these properties and sometimes you can change the properties. They are written as `Object.property`.

- **Single Quotes vs. Double Quotes**:
JavaScript doesn't care which you use, except when nesting. For instance, if you are dealing with a string of HTML code that contains quotes, be sure to balance them so the outer quotes are not used anywhere in the string. For instance:
`myCode = '<div id="myDiv">content here</div>'`

- **String**:
Strings are stored pieces of text. They are looked at as a group of characters.

- **Unobtrusive JavaScript**
A set of best practices for using JavaScript on a website. Under this paradigm, you should keep your JavaScript functionality and HTML markup completely separate and make sure all the content is available even if users have disabled JavaScript.

- **Variable**:
Variables hold information. They can hold numbers, text (strings), etc. When defining a variable, writing **var** before the variable name makes it local to that function. If you do not write **var**, then its value is global and accessible by all functions on the page.

JAVASCRIPT & JQUERY • COPYRIGHT NOBLE DESKTOP